D1111896

Contagious
Christian Living

Contagious Christian Living

with Study Guide

Joel R. Beeke

Preface by
Geoff Thomas

Reformation Heritage Books
and
Bryntirion Press

Published by
Reformation Heritage Books
2965 Leonard St., NE
Grand Rapids, MI 49525
USA
616-977-0599 / Fax 616-285-3246
e-mail: orders@heritagebooks.org
website: www.heritagebooks.org

and

Bryntirion Press
Bridgend
CF31 4DX
Wales, UK

Library of Congress Cataloging-in-Publication Data

Beeke, Joel R., 1952-
  Contagious Christian living : with study guide / Joel R.
Beeke ; preface by Geoff Thomas.
      p. cm.
  ISBN 978-1-60178-079-9 (pbk. : alk. paper)
  1. Christian life—Biblical teaching. 2. Christian life—
Textbooks. I. Title.
  BS680.C47B44 2009
  248.4—dc22

                              2009045552

Contents

Preface

Growing affection and trust characterize Joel Beeke's ministry at the annual Aberystwyth Evangelical Movement of Wales' Conference. Addressing 1200 people for a week of meetings for the third time,[1] the congregation is now in tune to the preacher from across the Atlantic. They appreciate the strands of his ministry, his thorough preparation, biblical exegesis, Calvinistic theology, and love for the Lord Jesus' person and work; his application of the Word to believers and unbelievers; his history of redemption insights; his personal reflections and anecdotes. His humor is manly and safe, welcome because of its rarity. Each year he seems to improve (though I have always enjoyed him), and I hear him with delight—though I am sure he would be the last person to recognize any "improvement."

Dr. Beeke also expresses his affection for the structure of the Conference; he is at ease with the singing and praying, the fact that the whole morning is characterized by first, a number of earnest prayer meetings, followed secondly by a single address

---

1. Addresses from the former two occasions have been published as *Portraits of Faith* and *Walking as He Walked*.

which the main speaker gives. So on four mornings in 2009 the theme of "Contagious Christian Living" was expounded. Anything less touchy-feely could not be imagined. These four messages, you will learn, center on Jesus Christ in the multifarious nature of his work, so that the themes are those of judgment, admonition, the call to repentance, and above all the proclamation of our Lord's free, accomplished redemption. The four messages are all aspects of the gospel, the good news that we are to preach always and exclusively, and they are models of that.

Dr. Beeke's concern was, by the Spirit's grace, to re-establish his hearers' proper relationship with God through our Savior, and by a newly discovered wonder at this achievement to encourage a fresh and living walk with God that would be contagious in the eyes of the church and world. Read these addresses for yourself and judge how successful our honored brother has been in his messages.

— Geoff Thomas

Introduction

When some people smile, they ignite smiles in people around them. They have contagious smiles. If that's what a contagious smile is, what is contagious Christian living? It is living that is so godly and so consistent that people around them cannot help but be impacted and inspired. Even unbelievers may be impressed with such consistency and purity, though they don't ultimately believe that Jesus Christ is the source of that life. Contagious Christian living is more than inspirational, of course, but it incites the same type of living in others.

Every metaphor breaks down at some point, and so does the term *contagious living*. The adjective *contagious* is helpful in describing Christian living, but we must not push it too far. People do not become Christians or live consistently holy lives simply because they are impressed with someone else's life. So it is not true that if you mix with godly people all the time, you will, by some sort of osmosis, automatically become godly. Some of the most wicked men and women who walk the earth spend much of their time surrounded by godly people, though they themselves are far from godly.

Osmosis is not the principal factor here; the Holy Spirit is. Children of God are "born, not of blood, nor of the will of the flesh, nor of the will of man, but of God" (John 1:13). They are not born by spending time with children of God. But the Holy Spirit does use means to accomplish his will, and one of the primary means he uses to influence unbelievers and believers is faithful Christians who lead godly lives. Most believers can trace their conversion, at least in part, to the influence of a godly person or persons in their lives. That's why the Puritan Thomas Watson says, "Association begets assimilation."

Three Prerequisites for Contagious Living

If this is the case, we should all strive to live contagious Christian lives, notable for their godliness. So how do you live such a life? Here are three prerequisites:

First, you must be a Christian. You might think that goes without saying, but it is very possible to attempt to live the Christian life without first settling the question of whether or not you are indeed a Christian.

If you were raised in a church, the error of assuming you are a Christian will be particularly easy to fall into. Everyone around you acts a certain way, so you act that way, too. Everyone around you says certain things about Jesus, so you say them, too. It is the only way of life you have ever known. But you do not become a Christian by saying and doing the things you see Christians doing; you become a Christian only when you wholeheartedly repent of sin and place all your hope, trust, and faith in Jesus Christ.

If you were not born in a church but joined one later in life and haven't been properly taught about justification by faith, you may think that acting like a Christian is the way to become a Christian. So before we talk about how to live a contagious Christian life, we must each ask ourselves, am I really a Christian? We can't even begin to live the life of contagious Christianity until we, by the Holy Spirit's grace, put all our trust in Jesus Christ and surrender ourselves to him.

Although it is an essential part, being a Christian isn't simply a matter of confessing Christ as Savior. It is also becoming totally dependent on Christ's grace. That Christ is the only Savior and Lord is an objective truth. But true Christians have this objective truth subjectively applied to their minds and hearts. Not only do they confess this objective truth; they have also experienced in their own lives the misery they were in because of their sin, the deliverance afforded to them by a willing and able Savior, and the gratitude and joyful service that flows out of that deliverance. Objective truth (truth "out there") becomes a subjective reality (truth "in the soul") that is fostered by spiritual disciplines.

Second, you must use the spiritual disciplines. Spiritual disciplines can be divided into four categories. The first category is private disciplines, such as reading and searching the Scriptures, meditation on biblical truths, private prayer, and journaling. The second category is domestic disciplines, such as family worship and godly conversation. The third is corporate disciplines, which include making diligent use of the preached Word and of the sacraments, seeking fellowship in the church, and sanctifying the Lord's Day. Fourth are neighborly disciplines, which include evangelizing and serving others, working for the well-being of God's kingdom, fleeing worldliness, and exercising stewardship over time and money.

When Christians exercise spiritual disciplines conscientiously and prayerfully, they grow in the grace and knowledge of Jesus Christ. He works in them what they need to truly live and grow as Christians. With that growth, the reality of Christianity breaks forth in godly fruit-bearing, which then becomes evident to everyone around them.

Third, you must develop an evangelistic heart. Such fruit-bearing is the beginning of a blessed and contagious Christian life. We begin to love others with the same kind of love that we received from God. We yearn for the spiritual welfare of others. We view every unconverted person as a mission field. We long to bring the gospel to unsaved people wherever we meet them. Hopefully, we love people so much that we learn to approach them as individuals. Sometimes that means using varied approaches in bringing the gospel. For one person, we may use the invitational approach of the Samaritan woman (John 4); for another, the testimonial approach of the blind man in John 9; for another, the convicting approach of Peter (Acts 2); for another, the intellectual approach of Paul (Acts 17); and for yet another, the service approach of Dorcas (Acts 9). Sometimes we will be drawn to use a combination of these approaches. All of these approaches depend on the character and need of the person as well as the promptings of the Holy Spirit.

The Challenges and Blessings of Living Contagiously

Do you really want to be a contagious Christian? Though this kind of living promotes purposeful, fulfilling, evangelistic, adventurous living, you should count the cost before asking God for it: it will demand a heavy investment of your time and energy, reading and study, sweat and tears, prayer and struggle. It will require your wholehearted commitment to serving God and others.

Though it offers permanent dividends, living a contagious Christian life is terrifically difficult and challenging. It includes the risk of embarrassment, rejection, failure, and even persecution (Matt. 5:11–12). It also requires a life of consistent godliness.

Oh, that we could all say with David Brainerd, "I care not where I live, or what hardships I go through, so that I can but gain souls to Christ. While I am asleep, I dream of these things; as soon as I awake, the first thing I think of is this great work. All my desire is the conversion of sinners, all my hope is in God."

What would happen throughout the world today if all Christians possessed such an evangelistic heart?

Perhaps you ask, "If becoming a Christian is based on Christ's performance, not ours, why should we go through the trouble and struggle of living such a life?" That question has been asked since the dawn of the Christian gospel. If salvation is in Christ alone through faith alone, why do good works?

The Heidelberg Catechism, a great Reformation document, provides a poignant answer to that question:

> Because Christ, having redeemed and delivered us by his blood, also renews us by his Holy Spirit, after his own image; so that we may testify, by the whole of our conduct, our gratitude to God for his blessings, and that he may be praised by us; also, that every one may be assured in himself of his faith, by the fruits thereof; and that by our godly conversation others may be gained to Christ (Q. 86).

There are many excellent reasons to do good works, but the one that specifically relates to contagious Christian living is "that by our godly conversation others may be gained to Christ."

A life of good works is blessed in many ways. People who live this way receive a blessing on their relationship with God (Ps. 128:4–5), their relationship to themselves (Ps. 7:8), their relationship with their family (Ps. 101:2; 128), their relationship with believers (Ps. 133), and their relationship with unbelievers (Dan. 6).

The Indispensability of the Spirit

Contagious Christian living brings many blessings, but let us always remember that the Holy Spirit is absolutely essential not only in empowering us to live contagiously but also in making that contagiousness effective by blessing others through our lives. Many believers forget that today; they write entire books on how to become a contagious person or a contagious church without mentioning (or scarcely so) the Holy Spirit. We must avoid this error at all costs. Godly lives do not automatically change others. Without the Holy Spirit's work in the hearts of those who come into contact with godly people, unbelievers may actually hate believers, finding them distasteful or even repulsive.

On the other hand, we must not negate the need for contagious Christian living. By his grace, the Holy Spirit can make the lives of godly Christians contagious in families, the church, and the marketplace. He does this not so much *because* of us, since we remain sinners and are not consistently godly, but he does this *in spite* of us. That is why the Belgic Confession says so powerfully and beautifully that God is not obliged to us for the good works that we do, but we are obliged to him (Art. 24). So the Holy Spirit is due all the glory for even the smallest degree of contagious Christian living. All such living is because of his abounding grace.

Are you living a contagious Christian life? Deep down, do you even want to become a contagious Christian? Do others look at you and say, "That's the way I want to live"? How, in dependence on the Holy Spirit, can you live a contagious life? To answer that, let us look at four people in the Bible who lived contagious lives. Let us examine how they became God's agents, how they were contagious, and what that contagious Christian living looks like. I pray God that the examination of their contagious lives may be used by the Spirit of God, if you are a Christian, to make your life more contagiously Christian, and if you are not yet saved, to move you to cry out to God for salvation and a truly contagious Christian life.

1

Sacrificial Submission
Jephthah's daughter (Judges 11:29–40)

Let us first look at Jephthah's daughter, whose story is told in Judges 11:29–40. Jephthah's daughter lived such a contagious life that she influenced many people in her day and for generations to come. Verse 40 says, "The daughters of Israel went yearly to lament the daughter of Jephthah the Gileadite four days in a year." They could not forget this daughter, for her life was a testimony of what God's grace can achieve in sinners such as us. By the Spirit's blessing, her sacrificial submission influenced many young women to surrender their lives in service to God.

Let us consider Jephthah's daughter's contagious sacrificial submission by first looking at the difficult circumstances that called for her submission. Next, we'll consider several ways in which this daughter showed sacrificial submission. Then we'll examine how her kind of sacrificial submission is still contagious today. Specifically, we will cover the difficult call for submission, the wonderful exercise of submission, and the inspiring contagiousness of submission.

The Difficult Call for Submission

God's plans often differ from ours. When this happens, we are faced with a choice: will we stubbornly proceed along the path we have mapped out for ourselves, or will we change course and follow the one God has laid before us? This choice can be difficult. You would love to play football with your friends on Thursday nights, but God is calling you to a ministry that is on Thursday nights. Which path will you take? You would love to have a career in law, but now God is calling you to motherhood. What path will you take?

This doesn't just go for career plans. We may have planned to spend the rest of our lives with the man or woman that we loved. But God took that man or woman from us. When God calls us to something we haven't planned, we must submit to his will, recognizing that it takes priority over our own and praying that our will would be conformed to his. That kind of submission is one of the toughest aspects of the Christian life. Yet it is precisely what Jephthah's daughter exhibited. She put aside her own plans—her own hopes and dreams—for the glory of God. And for many generations, the daughters of Israel commemorated her for her submission.

To understand Jephthah's daughter, we must first understand Jephthah and his vow.

The historical background of Jephthah's vow

Lest we consider the account of Jephthah and his daughter merely a tragic story about a foolish vow that cost the life of an innocent girl, let us examine the historical background of this incident.

God had brought the Israelites through the wilderness and into the promised land of Canaan. But they did not complete the conquest of the people there, as God had commanded them, and now they were living with the consequences. The people were being corrupted by the worship of strange gods. God brought judgment upon them by allowing other nations to conquer them and oppress them. After years of suffering, the children of Israel would cry out to God to save them. And he would. Throughout the book of Judges, God sent various leaders to rescue his people from destruction and oppression.

Jephthah was one of the judges whom God raised to lead the fight against oppressors. At first glance, Jephthah wasn't the kind of man you'd expect God to choose. He was the illegitimate son of a Gileadite and a prostitute. His half-brothers kicked him out of their father's house, and he was forced to live with a band of outcasts in the land of Tob.

Yet isn't this often the way that God works? He does not look for the cream of the crop to do his will; he looks for the downtrodden and the outcast so that by using them mightily he might receive all the glory. In Paul's words, God chooses "the foolish things of the world...the weak things of the world...the base

things of the world…the things that are despised…
yea, and things which are not" (1 Cor. 1:27–28) to do
his mighty works.

The elders of Gilead asked Jephthah to lead them
against the Ammonites who were amassed to fight
the Israelites. After some negotiations, Jephthah
agreed to do so. He sent messengers to the king of the
Ammonites. The king refused to listen so Jephthah
prepared his men to fight against the Ammonites.
As the battle was about to begin, Jephthah prayed
to God, making this vow: "If thou shalt without fail
deliver the children of Ammon into mine hands,
then it shall be, that whatsoever cometh forth of
the doors of my house to meet me, when I return in
peace from the children of Ammon, shall surely be
the LORD's, and I will offer it up for a burnt offering"
(Judg. 11:30–31).

How could Jephthah make such a foolish vow?
Didn't he have the foresight to think that someone he
loved might emerge from his house? Didn't he realize that he was making a promise that might mean
sacrificing his only child, his precious daughter?

Misunderstanding Jephthah's vow
Before jumping to conclusions, let us take a closer
look. When we do, we will discover that Jephthah did
not make a rash and foolish vow, and he did not offer
up his daughter as a burnt offering. This runs con-
trary to some old interpretations of this story. Some
commentators said that Jephthah lived in rough times

and was undoubtedly influenced by pagan ideas, which included human sacrifices and bribing gods with vows to obtain favors from them. According to this old view, Jephthah gave way to these pagan ideas and is therefore someone to be despised.

As we examine this story closely, however, there are eight matters in the context that, taken together, lead us away from supposing that Jephthah sacrificed his daughter.

• In the first place, Jephthah was not a rash man. Swearing that you will sacrifice whatever comes out of your house to meet you may be rash. But Jephthah had already proved to the elders of Gilead and the king of the Ammonites that he was a cautious man. He did not just jump at the request of the elders to become Israel's leader but carefully questioned them first to discover their motives and intentions. He did not rush headlong into battle, either, but sent messengers to the Ammonites in an attempt to find a diplomatic alternative to war and to plead the justness of Israel's cause.

• Second, in his discussions with the Ammonites, Jephthah demonstrated his familiarity with the Scriptures. Surely, then, he must have known that Leviticus 18:21 and Deuteronomy 12:29–32 prohibited offering human sacrifices—especially one's children—as an abomination before God. In addition, Judges 11 is set in the context of reformation. Israel, including Jephthah, had repented and was turning toward—not away from—the living God.

• Third, when Jephthah made his vow, the Spirit of the Lord was upon him. Would the Spirit inspire him to make a vow so clearly contradictory to the Spirit's own revealed Scripture? That is hard to believe, since the Word and the Spirit never contradict each other. It is also difficult to believe that Israel would have followed Jephthah as a leader if he had so flagrantly disobeyed Scripture and actually sacrificed his own daughter.

• Fourth, let us look closely at Judges 11:31, which says, "If thou shalt without fail deliver the children of Ammon into mine hands, then it shall be, that whatsoever cometh forth of the doors of my house to meet me, when I return in peace from the children of Ammon, shall surely be the LORD's, and I will offer it up for a burnt offering." A possible option for this translation is to remember that *burnt-offering* in Hebrew does not always mean blood-sacrifice. The word can also mean total dedication. In this case Jephthah's vow would have been: whatever comes out of my house "shall surely be the LORD's, and I will offer it for a complete dedication to the LORD."

Another translation issue hinders us from properly understanding the passage. The last verse of Judges 11 says the daughters of Israel went yearly to "lament" the daughter of Jephthah. The word translated here as "lament" is not translated this way anywhere else in the Bible. Rather it is understood elsewhere as to "rehearse" or "commemorate." So the daughters of Israel did not lament Jephthah's daughter's *death*. They commemorated her dedication to the service of God, which involved her wholehearted *submission*.

• Fifth, Jephthah had plenty of time after defeating the Ammonites and greeting his daughter to ponder what he would do next. He gave his daughter two months to bewail her virginity. Don't you think that if Jephthah really intended to sacrifice his daughter, priests from Shiloh would have come to him during that time to remind him of the divine prohibition of human sacrifice?

• Sixth, even if Jephthah's vow was rash, Leviticus 5:4–5 offered him the possibility of repenting of such a vow and Leviticus 27 the possibility that Jephthah could have redeemed his daughter by paying a ransom price. Yet Jephthah refused both of those options.

• Seventh, when Jephthah's daughter went to mourn for two months, she did not mourn her *impending death* but her *perpetual virginity* (Judg. 11:38).

• Finally, notice that Jephthah is commended rather than reprimanded in Scripture. He reigned over Israel for another six years. And 1 Samuel 12:11 names Jephthah as one who kept Israel safe. Would

Samuel have commended Jephthah if he had sacrificed his own daughter? More importantly, Hebrews 11:32 names Jephthah as a hero of faith rather than as a despicable pagan-like figure.

In conclusion, then, Jephthah was not vowing to kill his daughter but to dedicate her to the service of God, which involved the remarkable challenge of perpetual virginity. That is why verse 39 says he carried out his vow, but does not add, "and she died." Rather, it says, "she knew no man." Jephthah thus fulfilled his vow because his daughter lived the rest of her life as a virgin.

The remarkable challenge of Jephthah's vow
The vow that Jephthah took was not a trivial one, even though it did not mean killing his daughter. In Jephthah's day, a special order of women served in the tabernacle of God. They were not allowed to marry and have children. It seems that Jephthah dedicated his daughter to be one of those women. That is why the emphasis in the latter verses of Judges 11 is not on her death but on her perpetual virginity.

It is hard for us to grasp today what a great sacrifice Jephthah made in dedicating his daughter to God as a lifetime virgin. After all, Jephthah had only one daughter. If that daughter did not marry or have children, Jephthah's family line would not continue, which was a heavy cross for any male Israelite to bear. Even more importantly, Jephthah's family could never give birth to the Messiah, which is what every pious Israelite longed for. Jephthah's daughter also bore the burden of being unable to bear children in the lineage of the Messiah; in addition, for a woman to have no children at all was a sign of God's curse. Motherhood was the chief honor of womanhood.

While Jephthah and his daughter responded to this remarkable challenge with true submission, it is the daughter's submission that stands out as being particularly contagious. Let us take a closer look at this genuine Christian submission and its conta-giousness. What is true submission? How does it shape our lives? How is it contagious?

Jephthah's daughter teaches us that genuine Christian submission means, most simply, to bow under God's will and to be willing to give up any-thing for his glory. That is fairly easy to grasp. But the tougher question is: How do we, by the grace of the Holy Spirit, experience and exercise this as Chris-tians? Let us look closer at this issue.

The Wonderful Exercise of Submission

We don't learn the art of Christian submission in a day. Actually, we might more aptly speak of various degrees of submission. As in a stairway where the fifth step up is much farther than the first step, so true submission includes stages. At times, we may make more than one giant step of submission, but most of the time we experience submission as a variable process. We move downward in submission when we stop living close to God, and we move higher into submission as we come to depend more fully on him. Our growth in submission is not always certain. We progress in it more some days than others.

Jephthah's daughter, who was apparently very mature in grace, seemed to have progressed very far in submission. That, no doubt, is what made her faith so contagious that her dedication to the Lord was commemorated by the daughters of Israel. Let us look at five stages of submission, letting Jephthah's daughter be our mentor.

Acknowledge the Lord

The first step of submission is to *acknowledge the Lord* by saying, "It is the Lord!" Both Jephthah and his daughter immediately recognized that their affliction was from the hand of God. When his daughter walked out of the door of his home to meet him, Jephthah was very grieved, but he could not say, "I take back my vow." He recognized that God was intimately connected to the promise he had made. So Jephthah said, "I have opened my mouth unto the LORD, and I cannot go back" (v. 35). He was saying, "I have spoken to God, so God is speaking in this, God is active in my affliction, God is involved." Jephthah's daughter immediately echoed this thought in verse 36, saying, "Thou hast opened thy mouth *unto the LORD*."

Awareness of God is the beginning step of true, contagious, Christian submission. If we do not recognize the hand of God in our afflictions, we cannot submit to him. True submission does not blame the devil or man or fate or an accident for the ultimate source of its affliction but acknowledges the Lord as the primary source of all things, including our afflictions. True submission confesses: "I was dumb, I opened not my mouth; because thou didst it" (Ps. 39:9).

One of the great mottos of the Reformers was *coram Deo,* that is, "in the face, or presence, of God." It was a reminder that all of life must be lived in the consciousness that God is always here. Turn this motto inside out and we might say, "God is never not involved."

A few days after the bombing of the Twin Towers on September 11, Larry King interviewed three ministers and a rabbi. "Was God's hand in this tragedy?" King asked. Three of the four basically said, "No. God could have nothing to do with this." But John MacArthur said, "God has *everything* to do with this. He is involved." King then proceeded, and rightly so, to challenge the other three that the deity they professed must be impotent if he couldn't control such a tragedy.

How can you submit to a God who has nothing to do with your affliction? Such submission would be artificial and worthless. It would mean nothing. You could not go to God for help in such times because he would have no answer for your sorrow and difficulty. The very best you could do is "grin and bear it." What comfort would it be to believe in a God who could not comfort you in times of sadness and trial? Your life could never become contagious.

By contrast, the first thing you should remember when something awful happens to you is: "God is here; God is in this; it is the Lord!" Robert, age six, came to visit his grandfather, a professed atheist. The grandfather asked Robert to read a sign above his bed that said, "God is no where." Robert, who was just learning to read, struggled a bit. Not knowing the word *where*, he moved the "w" a little bit to the left, then read, "God is now here!" God used that incident to convict his grandfather of his sin. He repented of it before God and learned to follow him.

God is always here. Remembering that will keep you from much sin and teach you to let God be God. God sees us both in happy times and sad times; he knows what we are going through, and that is very comforting. It is great to know that God is always here to keep us from sin, but it is also wonderful to know that God is here when we are sick and in pain, for we know that he can help us.

The first step of submission, then, is to acknowledge that, no matter what happens in our lives, "It is the Lord!"

Justify the Lord

The second step of true submission is to *justify the Lord* by saying, "This is right! The Lord makes no mistakes." In verse 35, Jephthah said, "I cannot go back," implying, "It would not be right for me to break this vow. The Lord is righteous in all his ways." Jephthah's daughter basically said the same thing:

"Do to me according to that which hath proceeded out of thy mouth" (v. 36). She was saying, in effect, "This is right—right for you and righteous before God." She was also admitting she was an unworthy sinner who did not deserve the blessings of marriage and motherhood. Whatever happened to her would be under the righteous judgment of God.

Justifying the Lord in all that he does is a step up from simply acknowledging that he is present in a bad situation. It is one thing to say, "It is the Lord," and quite another to say, "It is right. I deserve it. I deserve even worse." Thus, when afflictions strike us, our first question is not, "Why *me?*" but "Why *not* me?"

The Scriptures repeatedly show us that justifying God in all his ways is a critical step of true faith and submission. When Samuel told Eli that his sons would be taken from him, Eli said, "It is the LORD: let him do what seemeth him good" (1 Sam. 3:18). When Absalom drove David from his throne, David said, "Behold, here am I, let him do to me as seemeth good unto him" (2 Sam. 15:26).

When I was twelve years old, I was upset with my mother because it seemed that no matter what I complained about she said that as sinners we deserved worse. Finally, in exasperation, I said, "You can say it could be worse about *anything!*"

Her response was, "That's right. Because we deserve hell, anything we receive above death and hell is only God's mercy. We have no reason to complain, *ever."* My mother was right: God is always mercifully righteous and just. Have you learned that, too?

Approve the Lord

The third step of true submission is to *approve the Lord* by saying, "It is well. The Lord's will is best."

Jephthah's daughter took this third step of submission. She was willing to have her father's vow fulfilled, even if it meant that she would bear the curse of perpetual virginity. So she said, "Forasmuch as the LORD hath taken vengeance for thee of thine enemies, even of the children of Ammon" (v. 36). In other words, "If the Lord's will is to exchange my perpetual virginity for the victory you received, Father, I approve of that. If that is God's will, it is good; yes, even best, for his will is always best. He knows what is good for me better than I do."

How contagious such approval of God's will is in the midst of affliction! Nothing quite impresses people so much as when believers *amen* the hard ways of God in their lives. When Job lost all ten of his children at once, he did not say, "But Lord, couldn't I keep at least one?" Rather, he approved God's way, saying, "The LORD gave, and the LORD hath taken away; blessed be the name of the LORD" (Job 1:21). Job fully approved of God's way with his children, even in their death. That is profound, contagious submission.

Church history is filled with martyrs who, in one way or another, said "it is well" as they went to their fiery deaths. Ignatius called the chains that bound him for being a Christian "sweet pearls" and reckoned suffering for the Lord Jesus an honor.

Have you ever been able to say in the midst of affliction that God knows what is best for you? Have you ever surrendered, gladly and willingly, all that you are and have to his holy, all-wise will?

Cling to the Lord
The fourth step of true submission is to *cling to the Lord* by saying, "If I perish, I perish, but I will cling to God's mercy." Isn't this precisely what Jephthah's daughter was saying when she asked her father in verse 37 that she might "go up and down upon the mountains, and bewail my virginity, I and my fellows"? True submission does not mean that you do not bewail your affliction, but it does mean that you cling to the Lord in your pain. That is what Jephthah's daughter did for two months. She engaged in submissive bewailing, not rebellious bewailing.

In true submission we cling to the Lord as our dearest friend, even when he seems to be coming against us as our greatest enemy. In a London park, I once saw a young woman repeatedly throw a ball at her dog. No matter how often or how hard the ball hit the dog, he quickly scooped it up and ran it back to his owner. The dog's entire demeanor was owner-centered. If you are truly submissive, you will suffer God's hardest blows and bring them to him as you cling to him afresh. You will say with Job, "Though he slay me, yet will I trust in him" (Job 13:15).

Honor the Lord

The most profound and highest step of true submission is to *honor the Lord* by saying, "His glory is greater than me and my salvation." This is where Jephthah's daughter excelled. She was so submissive that she would surrender anything rather than have God's name injured on her account. God's glory meant more to her than her own life. It is as if she said, "Father, do whatever you have vowed, for the glory of God is at stake. My future means nothing compared to the honor of God; I give up all for God's reputation."

Jephthah's daughter so identified with the cause of her father, which was the cause of the covenant-keeping God of Israel, that she was spiritually one with her father. She rejoiced in her father's safe return. The cause of God's people was so close to her heart that she was willing to approve whatever sacrifice the Lord asked of her so long as the people of God triumphed. Jephthah rent his clothes and was shaken when he saw his daughter, but she rejoiced and remained strong in faith because the Lord had remembered his covenant and vindicated the cause of his people. She no doubt had shed many tears while her father was battling the Ammonites; now that he was home, she was radiant with joy.

God's honor made her forget herself. She knew

that life's supreme goal and achievement was to honor God by acquiescing wholly to his will. What beautiful self-denial this daughter exercised!

We are so poor at self-denial today. We scarcely know what it means, much less experience the joys of exercising it. We do not realize that, without self-denial, we may possess everything without having a single particle of happiness. No wonder our lives are seldom contagious! John Calvin said the foundational fruit of our union with Christ is self-denial. What is more, it is the sacrificial dimension of true piety. For Calvin, self-denial meant realizing that we are not our own but belong to God. It meant yearning to focus our entire lives upon God, yielding everything we are and own to him as a living sacrifice. Then, whatever God does with us is good because it is his will.

A member of our church was scheduled for major surgery recently. Just before she was rolled into the operating room, I asked her, "How are you?"

She gripped my hand and said with confidence, "Whether we live, we live unto the Lord; and whether we die, we die unto the Lord: whether we live therefore, or die, we are the Lord's" (Rom. 14:8).

What a beautiful testimony of how grace can triumph in our souls! That is what Jephthah's daughter experienced. She lovingly bowed to her father under the sovereignty of God with calm acquiescence and holy self-forgetfulness. God meant far more to her than her own future. She did not reason or argue with God; the peace that passes all understanding overflowed within her. She was so absorbed in God that the devil could not shake her. She joyfully took up her cross and followed the Lord.

Jonathan Edwards once said, "The greatest moments of my life have not been those that have concerned my own salvation, but those when I have been carried into communion with God and beheld his beauty and desired his glory.... I rejoice and yearn to be emptied and annihilated of self in order that I might be filled with the glory of God and Christ alone." Similarly, Jephthah's daughter, for the sake of God's cause, actually rejoiced in the midst of her calamity and dashed dreams.

What are your hopes and dreams for the future? What one thing are you looking forward to? Would you give that up for the Lord and his reputation? Because of her father's vow, Jephthah's daughter would never know the joy of motherhood, and she would have to give up any thought of propagating a line that might give birth to the Messiah.

Jephthah also felt the pain of that loss. Fulfilling his vow meant that his family line would end and he would never have a place in the lineage of the Messiah. We sense Jephthah's struggle in verse 35 when he tore off his clothes and cried: "Alas, my daughter! Thou hast brought me very low!" He was willing to dedicate anything in his household to the service of the Lord, but did that have to be his only daughter?

Can you relate to such a loss? You pledge allegiance to Christ, you promise you'll go anywhere in his service, but does it have to be *there*? You'll do anything for him, but does it have to be *this*? You'd sacrifice anything for him, but does it have to be *that*?

The chief concern of Jephthah's daughter was to honor God and her father's faithfulness to his word. She was willing to sacrifice all her dreams to serve God in praise of the salvation he had provided from the Ammonites. Are you willing to make such a sacrifice?

The Inspiring Contagiousness of Submission

So, you see, the real issue is not how many afflictions we experience but whether those sorrows bring us into sweet submission before God as we surrender everything to him. Would you sacrifice your most cherished hopes and dreams if God asked you to? Jephthah's daughter did and set an example for thousands of Israelite girls after her. This young woman's willingness to give up marriage and sexual relations in submission to her father and to the providence of the Lord was contagious; successive generations of young Israelite girls looked up to her as an inspiring example. By the Spirit's grace, she inspired many to dedicate themselves to God's service.

If God sanctifies us, we will be most influential to others when we are most afflicted. People will watch us most closely then to see if and how faith sustains us.

David Livingstone (1813–1873), the great missionary, geographer, linguist, and campaigner against slavery, is a notable example of contagious Christian living. When Livingstone was a young boy, he had a close friend. The two of them spent much time together during which Livingstone was saved, whereas the other boy was not. Livingstone tried his utmost to convince his friend to turn to Christ. He knew that the best way to live was to sacrifice all for Christ, but his friend was convinced that the way to live was to pursue money and the pleasure and leisure that comes with it.

Livingstone went to Africa in sacrificial submission to the gospel and God's glory. His journeys to reach the unreached with the gospel took him thousands of miles on foot into remote African villages where no white person had ever been. Wherever he went, he preached.

When Livingstone died in Zambia at the age of sixty, his close friends buried his heart there while the embalmed remains of his body were brought to England, where he was given a state funeral at Westminster Abbey. Thousands of people lined the streets to pay homage to this great missionary and explorer.

A person in the crowd overheard a man in ragged clothes muttering under his breath as the hearse passed by: "You were right, Davey. You were right."

After the procession ended the onlooker asked the man in rags, "What did you mean by saying, 'You were right, Davey'"?

"David and I went to school together," the man said. "He tried to convince me to give up everything for Christ. I refused because I was sure that I could live a far better life if I pursued money. I spent my

life in the business world and eventually lost everything. Now I have nothing; no money and no friends.
I see now that Davey was right; he had everything
because he had God and he was willing to lay down
his life for a cause bigger than himself."

Are you, too, convinced that Davey was right? Will
you ask God for grace to be a contagious Christian of
sacrificial submission, like Jephthah's daughter and
David Livingstone? You may say, "This all seems so
impossible for me. You have set the bar far too high."

The bar *is* high, for two good reasons. First, too
many of us today who profess Christ set the bar too
low. We settle for mediocrity. We live far below our
privileges as Christians. The worldly sprinter strives
for excellence as he runs his race, but we Christians
too often sit on the sidelines, seldom making anyone
jealous of our Christian life and seldom witnessing
to anyone of the joy of knowing Jesus Christ as Savior and Lord. Shame on us for making the gospel so
banal, so mediocre, so distasteful!

The second reason for setting the bar high is that
God can give you the grace to live this way because
of his Son, who is the supreme and perfect example
of sacrificial submission. Even when he was twelve
years old, Jesus was busy doing his Father's business
(Luke 2:49). He always lived *coram Deo*, always justified his Father, always approved of his Father, always
clung to his Father, and always honored his Father.
Even in the dark night of his soul, Jesus reached out
for God, saying from the depth of his being, "My

God, my God, why hast thou forsaken me?" Let us learn from Jesus, who was meek and lowly for our sakes, so that we, by grace, may live contagious lives of sacrificial submission.

We will not live perfect lives. We may often stumble. But by the grace of the Holy Spirit, and for Christ's sake, we can live contagiously. And we can testify to ourselves and to others that the only way to live, the purposeful way to live, the joyous way to live is to live contagiously for the glory of God alone, in Christ alone, by faith alone, through grace alone! *Soli Deo Gloria!*

2

Christ-centeredness

Bartimaeus (Mark 10:46 –52)

"Is he a Christ-preacher?" That is the question often asked in the Netherlands to evaluate a minister in many Reformed circles. If you can say, "Yes, my minister is a Christ-preacher," you are saying at least four things:

- Being a Christ-preacher is the most fundamental calling of a minister of the gospel. If a minister is not a Christ-preacher, he really is no preacher at all. He may be a teacher or a lecturer, but he is not a preacher. He has failed in everything.

- Being a Christ-preacher means that he is determined, like Paul, to preach "Jesus Christ and him crucified" in every sermon. It means that he strives to preach the Savior biblically, doctrinally, experientially, and practically in all his grandeur as Savior and Lord; in Scripture's revelation of who he is in the more than 250 names ascribed to him; in the mystery of his natures as transcendent Jehovah and immanent man; in his offices as teaching prophet, compassionate priest, and eternal king; in his humiliation and his exaltation; and in his roles in salvation, being the wisdom, justification, sanctification, and complete redemption of his people (1 Cor. 1:30).

- Being a Christ-preacher means that he preaches the gospel, not just intellectually, but also from the heart. He has a personal, existential knowledge of the Savior. In the depths of his soul, he understands John 17:3, the precious text that John Calvin kept returning to in so many of his writings: "And this is life eternal, that they might know thee the only true God, and Jesus Christ, whom thou hast sent."

- Being a Christ-preacher is the foundational mark of being a Spirit-anointed preacher, for the Spirit's preeminent work is to glorify Christ by revealing him to sinners. The implication is that if Christ is not at the center of your pastor's preaching, his preaching will do little good, and his ministry will not be contagious.

The same type of question might be applied to everyone: "Are you a Christ-centered believer?" Do you know Christ biblically, doctrinally, experientially, and practically? Does everything in you need to find him, follow him, and glorify him? If so, you are a contagious Christian. If you do not know Christ experientially, you are not saved and not contagious. You may be a nominal Christian, but your faith is of no value. You are failing in everything that truly matters because you are still dead in your trespasses and sins.

To understand contagious Christianity, let us look at a character you might not initially think of as a contagious Christian. He is Bartimaeus, a blind man, who became a contagious Christian by Christ's grace. In our study of Bartimaeus, we will look at the contagiousness of being Christ-centered from Mark 10:46–52 and Luke 18:43, which says, "And immediately he received his sight, and followed him, glorifying God: and all the people, when they saw it, gave praise unto God."

Let's look, then, at Christ-centered contagiousness through three traits of Bartimaeus: needing Jesus, finding Jesus, and following and glorifying Jesus.

Needing Jesus

On an early afternoon in the spring, Jesus Christ and his disciples approached the historic city of Jericho. For the last time Jesus would cross the Jordan River. Ahead of him, only fifteen miles away, lay Jerusalem, where he knew he would be crucified. Jesus was on his way to death.

Jericho was between Jordan and Jerusalem. It was the city that Joshua conquered first upon entering Canaan, the land God had promised to his people. After Jericho was destroyed by Joshua, a divine curse was pronounced upon anyone who rebuilt the city. When Hiel the Bethelite attempted to rebuild Jericho, God's curse came upon him: he lost his oldest and his youngest sons while restoring the walls of Jericho. Later, the prophets Elijah and Elisha established a school for prophets at Jericho. Elisha miraculously healed the waters of Jericho by throwing salt into it.

By the time of Jesus, Jericho had become the headquarters of rich publicans. Herod built magnificent walls around the city, and Archelaus planted beautiful gardens within it. Jericho became so lush that it was known as the Eden of Palestine.

As Jesus moved through Jericho, a large crowd accompanying him, something more beautiful than all the external beauty of Jericho transpired. He saved two sinners: a very rich man named Zacchaeus and a very poor man named Bartimaeus. Both were converted, showing that the power of Jesus is not confined to one class of people. His saving work can break the heart of the wealthiest as well as the poorest people. How beautifully the gospel transcends classes, races, and other divisions that people make among themselves! As Galatians 3:28 says, "There is neither Jew nor Greek, there is neither bond nor free, there is neither male nor female: for ye are all one in Christ Jesus."

Both Zacchaeus and Bartimaeus were called by

sovereign grace to salvation in Jesus Christ. Zacchaeus went out to see Jesus and came back home
with Jesus. He went out to get a glimpse of Jesus with
his eyes and came back with Jesus in his heart (Luke
19:3–6). In a moment, the proud robber became the
penitent alms-giver (v. 8). Zacchaeus would never
forget the night that Jesus stayed at his home and
assured him that he had become a true son of Abraham (v. 9).

The second conversion took place outside of Jericho. A poor beggar was sitting by the roadside, asking
for handouts. Day after day, he sat beside the road
leading out of Jericho. He was totally dependent on
the generosity of passersby to eke out a living. That
day, no one gave him anything. People were deaf to
this beggar's plaintive cry for alms.

A beggar is always a sad sight, but Bartimaeus
was particularly pitiful because he was blind. Poverty
and blindness often went together in Jesus' day. It
wasn't uncommon for the fine dust that filled the air
with the slightest breeze to afflict those who worked
in the field with an eye disease that culminated in
blindness.

So poor, blind Bartimaeus sat by the road. Mark
10:46 says, "As he [Jesus] went out of Jericho with
his disciples and a great number of people, blind Bartimaeus, the son of Timaeus, sat by the highway side
begging." I do not think any of us would be willing to
trade places with Bartimaeus. But do you realize that
by nature we are just as wretched, spiritually speak-

ing, as that beggar if we are not saved? We may not be materially poor or physically blind, but if we are not born again, we are spiritually poor and spiritually blind.

In Adam, our covenant-head in Paradise, we were rich in God. Our vision was not the slightest bit impaired. We saw everything in the right light. We were created in God's image, endowed with knowledge as his prophets, with righteousness as his priests, and with holiness as his kings. But then, in Adam, we willfully and voluntarily sinned against God, transgressing the covenant and the commandments of God. The result was that we now are born into this fallen world as spiritually blind and poor. We are spiritually blind because sin has darkened our understanding, and blindness has alienated us from the life of God. Paul says, "The natural man receiveth not the things of the Spirit of God: for they are foolishness unto him; neither can he know them, because they are spiritually discerned" (1 Cor. 2:14). Our spiritual blindness is as incurable as was Bartimaeus's blindness in his day.

Have you ever felt so spiritually blind that you could not see the danger you were in? Did you cry to God for spiritual sight? Are you still spiritually blind today? How can you know for sure?

God offers us great realities in his Word. He offers us the realities of himself, sin, heaven, hell, and eternity. By nature, we are blind to those. We are blind to the threats of God against the heinousness of sin.

We are blind when the curses of the broken law do not terrify us, when the promises of the gospel do not touch us, and when we see no beauty in Christ to long for him. We are blind when we see no glory in the gospel, no value in salvation, and no beauty in holiness.

In spite of all our material goods, we are spiritually poor when we are spiritually blind. Too often, however, we don't realize that. We are often like the church of Laodicea that Jesus said thought it was rich and needed nothing when it was really "wretched, and miserable, and poor, and blind, and naked" (Rev. 3:17). We are poor when we do not know Jesus as our only comfort in life and in death, when we lack Jesus' righteousness, which is the only righteousness that can justify us. We are poor without the Holy Spirit, who alone works true conversion in us. We are poor without the inner peace of conscience, true happiness in this life, joy for the life to come, and the title to a heavenly inheritance. We are poor without God, without hope in this world, without saving interest in the covenant of promise. We are poor when we have no Surety for our debts, no Intercessor to pray for us, no Advocate to plead our case. We are poor when we are exposed to the wrath of God and the Lamb and are unprepared for death, judgment, and eternity.

By nature, we sit side by side with Bartimaeus, begging for what the world has to offer, such as honor, profit, and respect. And those are but pennies. Our real problem is that, though we are not ashamed to beg from the world, we are too proud to bow before God. Have you ever seen yourself as a beggar before God, pleading to know Jesus as Savior of your soul? That is what happened to Bartimaeus.

Bartimaeus raised his head when he heard a great multitude coming. When he asked what was going on, he was told that Jesus of Nazareth was passing by (Luke 18:37). This was the last time Jesus would pass by Bartimaeus. What an opportunity! Would Bartimaeus call for help? If you are not yet saved, today may be your last opportunity to respond to Christ. Will you call out for mercy?

No doubt Bartimaeus often had heard how Jesus of Nazareth cured lepers, made the deaf hear, delivered people possessed by demons, and even raised people from the dead. He had also heard how Jesus opened the eyes of the blind.

But this time when Bartimaeus heard "Jesus of Nazareth passeth by," the Holy Spirit made those words come alive in his heart. When he heard those words, hope sprang up as he asked himself, "Is it possible that Jesus would be merciful to me as well?"

In those moments, the light of God shone in Bartimaeus. Convicted of his sin and the reality of judgment, he felt such a need for Jesus that, as Mark 10:47 says, "He began to cry out."

True Christianity usually begins with such a cry. Just as crying out is a sign of life in a newborn baby, so crying out is a sign of spiritual life in a newborn Christian. We know that Bartimaeus's crying out was the fruit of the Holy Spirit because he said, "Jesus, thou Son of David, have mercy on me" (v. 47). His cry was not, "open my physical eyes," but "have mercy on me." That shows what was going on in Bartimaeus. Though he was concerned about receiving physical sight, his primary concern was spiritual; he cried out for mercy.

There are four reasons this was so. First, just as crying is the sign of life in a newborn, so the Holy Spirit's work in a sinner begins with repentance. Under conviction, the sinner learns to cry out from the depths of his soul because of sin. Second, Bartimaeus only asked for mercy, without citing any merits or excuses. He did not say, "Have mercy on me because I can't help it that I am blind and poor." He prayed the publican's prayer, "O God, be merciful to me a sinner," which Jesus said sent the man to heaven justified. Third, Bartimaeus could not let Jesus pass by without calling for mercy. He could not leave Jesus alone. Fourth, though the people told Bartimaeus that Jesus of Nazareth was passing by, Bartimaeus called out to Jesus as "Son of David," which is a messianic title. Evidently the Holy Spirit convinced Bartimaeus of who Jesus really was. These are all hopeful signs that the Spirit was beginning to work salvation in Bartimaeus's soul.

Have you ever cried out to God because of your sin? Have you asked for mercy without citing any merits of your own or any excuses for sin? Can you let Jesus pass by with all his invitations and exhortations without crying out? Have you ever truly called on Jesus as the Messiah?

By calling out to Jesus as Son of David, Bartimaeus declared to the multitude around him who Jesus truly was. It was as if he said, "Jesus, Son of David, long-promised Messiah and Prophet of righteousness, King of kings, have mercy on me." By faith, Bartimaeus believed that Jesus was the great Deliverer, but his concern was: "Will he deliver me? I know he is able, but is he willing to deliver such a poor, blind beggar as I?"

Bartimaeus faced many obstacles. Not only was he poor and blind, but the crowd made matters difficult for him. Verse 48 says, "Many charged him that he should hold his peace." They did not appreciate Bartimaeus's cries for a variety of reasons. Some were opposed to the beggar's blatant reference to Jesus as the Messiah. Some were embarrassed by this blind man who sat in the shadows of their wealthy city. Some felt it was improper for Bartimaeus to shout at a prophet, even if he was from a despised place like Nazareth. And some were eager to get to Jerusalem for the Passover and did not appreciate being delayed.

So they rebuked, censured, and even threatened Bartimaeus, in effect saying, "If you continue carrying on like this, we will stop you. So close your mouth or be prepared to suffer the consequences."

Likewise, many people today try to shut the mouths of those who cry out for Jesus. They say, "You're okay as you are. Maybe you need a little therapy, but you don't need Jesus. Christianity is just fanaticism."

But Bartimaeus could not stop crying out. Jesus was his only hope. So the blind man did not hold his peace, but, as verse 48 says, he "cried the more, a great deal." The streets rang with his shouts, "Son of David, have mercy on me. Have mercy, Lord, or I perish."

When sinners cry out for Jesus, Satan can raise many objections. Why bother calling for Jesus? He won't help you, anyhow. You are blind; you don't really know what you are asking for. You are a beggar; you don't deserve to be saved. You have sinned too much; why would the Son of God offer you anything? Jesus saves only the elect; you cannot possibly be one of them.

Has Jesus ever become an absolute necessity for you, so that you could not but cry out for him no matter how many obstacles you encountered? Then, like Bartimaeus, you are close to finding him!

Finding Jesus

Bartimaeus cried to Jesus as the Messiah whom Isaiah had prophesied would open the eyes of the blind. However, Jesus did not immediately respond to the beggar. He waited to try the faith of Bartimaeus so that he would cry all the more, "Son of David, have mercy on me."

Jesus heard Bartimaeus's cry. He heard his cry from eternity when he had already determined to

work that cry in the beggar's heart. Jesus also heard
Bartimaeus in time. In the middle of a noisy crowd,
while on his last journey to Jerusalem where he
would drink his Father's bitter cup of wrath and suffer a baptism of blood, Jesus heard Bartimaeus. On
this most important journey of his life, when Jesus
was to bear the sins of his people to satisfy God's
justice, to vindicate the truth of God, to reveal the
eternal love of God, and to magnify the law of God—
a journey that would impact heaven and earth and
hell—Jesus heard the prayer of a blind beggar.

What an encouragement that is for sinners
today! If Jesus heard blind Bartimaeus in the middle of a crowd, when the weight of the wrath of his
Father and the sins of his people were about to press
down on him, how much more, today, when he has
ascended to the Father's right hand and has his ears
tuned to the earth to hear the faintest whisper, will
he not hear the cry of a spiritual beggar? Would he
who heard the cry of the poor in the depths of his
humiliation not hear their cry in the height of his
exaltation?

Verse 49 says, "Jesus stood still." The crowd was
shocked into silence. Why was Jesus stopping? Would
he, too, command Bartimaeus to hold his peace?

Jesus stands still yet today when his people cry
out to him from the depths of their soul. A precious,
unforgettable day was dawning for Bartimaeus. For
when Jesus stands still beside needy sinners, good
news is at hand. He stands still to love and deliver

sinners, in fulfillment of Ezekiel 16:8, which says, "When I passed by thee, and looked upon thee, behold, thy time was the time of love."

Jesus hears and stands still, but he also calls. Verse 49 says, "Jesus commanded him to be called." Here before a beggar, Jesus modeled the Great Commission before formally stating it to his disciples. What a mission statement this is for the church and every believer today; it commands us to call everyone we meet to come to Jesus!

Bartimaeus feared that Jesus would pass by him without stopping. He expected that. He knew he was unworthy to be called by Jesus. But then someone said to him, "Be of good comfort, rise; he calleth thee" (v. 50). Jesus the Messiah, the Son of David, was calling the beggar. Oh, what a sacred, unforgettable moment!

The command was irresistible, for it came from Jesus' own mouth. Bartimaeus could not stay where he was. Verse 50 says, "And he, casting away his garment, rose, and came to Jesus." Bartimaeus cast aside his outer garment, which was probably a loose, foot-catching robe. No doubt it was the costliest thing he owned, but it was a hindrance for him to come to Jesus. Bartimaeus's need was so urgent that he did not take the time to gather up his outer garment and tuck it in his belt. Rather, he got rid of the garment altogether in his haste to reach the Savior. He needed Jesus *now!*

This outer garment is symbolic of anything that

may hinder us from coming to Jesus. It is also a symbol of pride, for though the poor in Jesus' day may have owned such a robe, they scarcely had anything else. Bartimaeus did not care what people thought of him. He gladly cast away the most beautiful thing he owned to come in his shabby, beggarly clothes to Jesus. His outer garment was a filthy rag to him compared to the beauty of Jesus Christ. In those moments, his outer garment lost all its value for it was an obstacle to his coming to Christ.

Have you ever been stripped of pride to come to Jesus? Have you cast away all human merit and value to come to him? Have you put aside as nothing your religious righteousness to be unimpeded by any obstacle to come to Jesus as a needy beggar? Have you cast away every hindrance to flee to Jesus so he could clothe you with his white-robed righteousness and become your all-in-all?

Then you know what it means to be drawn by cords of love and mercy to Jesus. His indescribable power has made you rise and go to Jesus. You could not stay away any longer. You could not come fast enough, for Jesus was your only desire in heaven and on earth. Just like Bartimaeus, you came to Christ by faith despite every obstacle.

In spite of his blindness, trials, and doubts, Bartimaeus came in emptiness to Jesus to receive his fullness. From eternity, Jesus had found Bartimaeus, and now in time, Bartimaeus found Jesus.

"What wilt thou that I should do unto thee?"

Jesus asked the beggar (v. 51). Jesus already knew the answer, of course, but he asked the question for the sake of Bartimaeus and the crowd. He asked it for Bartimaeus to strengthen his faith, and for the crowd, so that the beggar's faith in declaring the true desire of his heart would be contagiously winsome to them.

Bartimaeus immediately answered: "Lord, that I might receive my sight" (v. 51). In the original Greek, Bartimaeus addressed Jesus as "Rabboni," which means "my Lord," "my Master," or "my Teacher." By faith, he was openly declaring to the multitude that Jesus was not just a prophet from Nazareth but his Master and Lord and Teacher, to whom he was willing to subject his entire life.

The word *rabboni* implies various levels of teachers. A *rab* was a student who was training to become a doctor of law. A *rabbi* was a doctor of law. *Rabbin,* the plural form of *rabbi,* were the chief Jewish authorities on matters of law and doctrine. *Rabboni* was an endearing term for a supreme or divine teacher. Bartimaeus and Mary Magdalene were the only people in the New Testament who called Jesus, Rabboni. When Jesus tenderly spoke Mary's name at his empty sepulcher, she turned and cried out to him in that moment of sacred encounter, "Rabboni!" (John 20:16).

Bartimaeus likewise experienced a moment of sacred encounter with Christ. By calling out "Rabboni," Bartimaeus was declaring that Jesus was Lord of lords and Teacher of teachers. Though his request included the freedom to see with his physical eyes, in the highest sense he was asking for something more profound. He was saying, as it were, "Rabboni, my dear divine Savior and Master, grant me physical sight, but also open my heart's eyes so that I may be healed of spiritual misery and my sins may be washed away. Rabboni, let me receive spiritual eyesight so that I may truly see thy salvation."

Jesus' reply was simple and profound: "Go thy way; thy faith hath made thee whole" (v. 52). The Greek word for "whole" that is used here means a well-rounded, fulsome wholeness. It is as if he was saying, "I have healed you, both physically and spiritually. I have made you whole. Now you are free to go." Bartimaeus was made whole in every area of life. He was made whole inside and out, spiritually and physically. He received that wholeness by faith, which is the gift of God (Eph. 2:8). True saving faith is the means God uses to bring a sinner to Jesus. Bartimaeus came to Christ by faith prompted by the Holy Spirit and was healed. Jesus graciously told Bartimaeus his faith had healed him, even though that faith was a gift of Jesus. Jesus was right to do so, however, for Bartimaeus did exercise this faith.

Let me illustrate how that works. When my children were young, my wife would come to me a few weeks before my birthday, and say, "The children want to get you a gift for your birthday, so will you give me some money?" I would give my wife money, which she would then give to my children, who were too young to have money of their own. They would buy a gift and give it to me on my birthday. I would not respond to that gift by saying, "Thank you for my gift, which you got with my money!" The gift was theirs because they had played an active role in buying the gift, even if they had used my money. The gift was theirs. So, I said, "Thank you so much for *your* wonderful gift to me."

Similarly, Jesus said to Bartimaeus, "*Thy* faith hath made thee whole." Jesus was simply being gracious in speaking about his own gift to Bartimaeus, which Bartimaeus was privileged to exercise. And in that moment, blessed Bartimaeus was made whole. We read, "Immediately he received his sight" (v. 52). He could see, and the first person he saw was Jesus! What unspeakable joy must have flooded his soul!

What impression this healing must also have made on the crowd! Did the Spirit bless this sacred encounter to any of those souls? Was the faith of Bartimaeus contagious for them?

Is it contagious for you? Do you know the joy of having the scales of unbelief fall from your eyes so that you can see Jesus by faith? Then you saw light in Jesus' light, didn't you? Suddenly, you realized that he was the secret of life. You found everything in him. He became your Son of righteousness and your salvation. You could say with the blind man who was healed in John 9:25, "One thing I know, that, whereas I was blind, now I see," and with Paul in Philippians

3:8, "I count all things but loss for the excellency of the knowledge of Christ Jesus my Lord."

Following and Glorifying Jesus

When Jesus said, "Go thy way," Bartimaeus did not go away. He could not, for he was bound to Jesus. He had tasted the faith that finds freedom in Christ and which freely binds itself to Jesus. The love of Christ constrained Bartimaeus to follow Jesus.

Bartimaeus followed Jesus gladly. Choosing between Jesus and his old friends and old way of life was no contest. It was like comparing light to darkness or life to death. Bartimaeus was compelled to surrender everything to his Rabboni. He was irresistibly drawn by the Good Shepherd who said, "my sheep hear my voice, and I know them, and they follow me" (cf. John 10). He became a disciple of Jesus with his whole heart.

Verse 52 says he "followed Jesus in the way." What way? The way to Jerusalem, the way to the cross, the narrow path of salvation, the way that Jesus demands of all his followers. Jesus says in Matthew 16:24: "If any man will come after me, let him deny himself, and take up his cross, and follow me." It is not an easy or painless way. As Bunyan says in *Pilgrim's Progress*, it is the way that involves climbing the Hill Difficulty and descending into the Valley of Humiliation.

Following Jesus is challenging. For people of flesh and blood, it is impossible in themselves to follow Christ. But by grace, the way of Christ becomes a blessed and contagious way. Bartimaeus became willing in the moment of healing to be Rabboni's servant. As Paul says, he became the *doulos,* or willing slave of Jesus forever. He was willing to surrender his entire life unconditionally to his wonderful master, Rabboni.

When others see us unconditionally following Jesus, they may be won to Christ by our godly demeanor. Has God humbled you by showing you that the grace he gave you to follow him has motivated others to follow him? Contagious living does not make us proud; it profoundly humbles us. We realize that everything we have received has been given to us by Jesus; therefore, we have no cause for boasting. God must receive all the glory.

So Bartimaeus followed Jesus, "glorifying God" (Luke 18:43). Bartimaeus did not just follow Jesus; he glorified him. As he followed, he glorified Christ. He could not remain silent, even if his friends rejected him, Pharisees despised him, or Sadducees threatened him. None of that was important. Bartimaeus could only speak to others about how wonderful Jesus was.

Can't you picture him talking to the Pharisee on his right and on his left, whoever would listen? "Let me tell you how amazing Jesus is. He is the long-awaited Messiah, the Son of God, the Lord of glory. He is my Rabboni. I will be his willing slave for the rest of my life. I was a beggar by the wayside, but now Jesus has done everything for me. He opened my physical eyes. He opened my spiritual eyes. I am a new creation. I have no idea why he did this because I do not deserve it, but I now have joy, purpose, and meaning in life. If he can do this for me, he can do it for anyone—he can do it for you! Just cry out to him and go to him as you are. He will save you."

Do you, too, relish opportunities to speak about Jesus, to sing his praises to people around you? Is your conversation filled with Christ? Jesus says, "Out of the abundance of the heart the mouth speaketh" (Matt. 12:34). Does your mouth speak of Christ because your heart is filled with him? Have you felt like Bartimaeus after his encounter with Jesus? Do you still feel like that, or have you lost your first love? Do you glorify God? When is the last time you have spoken to someone about Jesus?

But how do we glorify God? We glorify God by confessing our sins to God and fleeing to Christ for forgiveness. We glorify him by praising, worshiping, and delighting in the triune God as Creator, Provider, and Redeemer. We glorify him by trusting God and surrendering everything we have and are into his hands. We glorify him by being zealous for his glory; by walking humbly, thankfully, and cheerfully before God; and by becoming increasingly conformed to the image of his Son. We glorify him by knowing, loving, and living the commands of God's Word and by being heavenly minded. We glorify him by cherishing the desire to be with him forever and by having his glory as our highest ambition, our most profound purpose, and our deepest joy.

There is no better way to be contagious than to glorify God with our walk and our talk. Our walk is most important. If we walk worldly and talk godly, the contradiction will cause irreparable damage. Like the Pharisees who talked much but lived little of what they taught, we would be more contagious for ill than for good. The old adage rings true that though your walk talks and your talk talks, your walk talks more than your talk talks. So Luke says that when the crowd of people *saw* that Bartimaeus followed Christ, they "gave praise unto God" (Luke 18:43).

That is not to say that Bartimaeus's talk was unimportant. A godly walk that is not reinforced by godly conversation will lack considerable clarity and contagiousness. No doubt what the people saw was that Bartimaeus's walk and talk complemented one another. And so they praised God.

Maybe you ask, "But how can I talk to someone evangelistically? I don't know what to say!" Begin by getting to know that person a bit. Show interest and love. Find out who he or she has as family members and what he or she does for work. Find out where your new friend went to school and what his or her foremost interests and hobbies might be. Most individuals will gladly tell you such things when you express interest with caring and loving questions. In turn, he or she will most likely begin to ask you questions, giving you the opportunity to say, in a word, that Christ means everything to you.

Then you can approach this person gently with questions about church and God. When he or she feels your love, it won't be long before you can ask, "Do you have a personal, saving relationship with Jesus Christ?" or "Have you been born again?" or any question of that sort. Just last week when I asked this question of a young woman, she told me that at a Youth Camp a few years ago, she was asked by her supervisor if she was converted, and when she said that she was not, the supervisor ever so gently asked her, "When you are brought to stand before God on the Judgment Day, what excuse will you use for remaining unconverted?" That question haunted this young woman for several days, until the Holy Spirit penetrated her soul with it and used it for her genuine conversion. Amazing grace: God can use one evangelistic question to reap a regeneration from the dead!

The Holy Spirit uses both our walk and our talk to impact others for good. He used Bartimaeus as he followed Jesus with his steps and proclaimed Jesus with his mouth. The people then praised God, some no doubt truly, and others perhaps only because Bartimaeus was no longer physically blind. They were delighted with the miracle. For some, the contagiousness of Bartimaeus had only outward effects; for others, it also had inward effects. It was not up to Bartimaeus to separate these two groups.

The beauty of the Christian life is that though

God will sometimes use us to impact people only outwardly, at other times he will use us to win people to Christ. It is up to God to decide how he will use us. We are called to live contagious Christian lives, but only God can use that to draw others to Christ. Often, the people that we are sure will never be influenced by us, are; and those we think we might influence, are not. God is sovereign. Our task is simply to sow the good seed of the Word wherever we go, glorifying God in our homes, at work, at school, on the airplane, and in the marketplace, trusting that God will use that as he deems fitting. We must do the sowing; God does the fruit-bearing. One day, in eternity, God will reveal that the fruit-bearing was far more than we ever realized, to the praise of his glory.

So what about you? Is your life contagious? I'm afraid that some of you are not living contagious lives because you do not truly know Jesus. You have not been born again. You go to church and perhaps read your Bible every day, but you live with little, if any, true consciousness of God in your lives. You are not Christ-centered. You are spiritually dead.

Jesus is passing by you today. He still offers you an opportunity to cry out. He is passing by you in sermons; are you listening? He passes by you in Bible study; do you understand him? He passes by you in sickness and in health; are you taking his healing and mercy to heart? He passes by you in prosperity and adversity; do you hear his voice? He passes by you in your family, at work, in your nation; do you see his footsteps?

As he passes by, he calls: "Today, if ye will hear his voice, harden not your heart. Behold, now is the accepted time, behold, now is the day of salvation. Repent, repent! Behold, I stand at the door and knock."

How much longer Jesus will pass by you, I do not know. All I know is that it is not yet too late for you to cry out for mercy. The day will come soon when he will no longer pass by, and you must be prepared to meet him. You do not know when you will die.

Now is the time to cry out, "Jesus, Son of David, have mercy on me that I may receive my sight." Do not be like the rich young ruler who turned away from Jesus because he was unwilling to cast away everything he owned to follow Jesus. Rather, make haste to come to Jesus for your life's sake. Time is short, but eternity is forever. Do not let Jesus pass you by without crying out to him. You will not be sorry.

3

Contagious Blessing

Jacob's Peniel (Genesis 32:22–32)

Jacob was not a very nice person. His very name means twister or deceiver, which revealed his conniving character. That cunning character often became a snare to him. In his youth, Jacob, the second-born twin, pressed his first-born twin, Esau, for the rights of the firstborn son. Later, Jacob deceived his blind father to obtain Esau's blessing, even using the name of God to get it. In the holiest of things, Jacob lied and deceived.

Jacob's craftiness backfired on him. He was forced to leave his parents without friends and without possessions, except for a staff and a cruse of oil. He could scarcely have been poorer. He crossed over the Jordan River as he left the land of promise. Behind him, he left a cursing brother and weeping parents. Everything seemed hopeless. Jacob was miserable. What future did he have as a homeless man?

Astonishingly, the Lord blessed Jacob in his need. At Bethel, where Jacob stopped for the night,

God revealed himself to Jacob, assuring Jacob that he, the faithful, covenant-keeping Lord, would be with Jacob. After Jacob traveled a long distance, the Lord led Jacob to his mother's family. Jacob found a home, a job, and a woman to love, and the Lord blessed Jacob's work. Though Jacob's uncle and employer changed Jacob's wages ten times, Jacob continued to prosper.

After Jacob served his uncle twenty years, God—who didn't want Jacob to get too comfortable away from the Promised Land—commanded Jacob to return to Canaan. By that time, Jacob was rich in family and possessions. God had pursued Jacob in his wanderings and blessed him.

Jacob obeyed God's command to pack up and leave. When his uncle, Laban, pursued and overtook Jacob at Mount Gilead, God wonderfully intervened. In the hill country of Gilead (Mahanaim), angels reassured Jacob that God would protect him against Laban and against Esau, who was now coming after Jacob with a militia of four hundred men.

The night before meeting Esau, Jacob was driven to his knees in prayer. His humble, sincere, beautiful prayer is recorded in Genesis 32:9–12. In it, Jacob pleads for help on the basis of God's covenant, God's command, God's promise, God's mercy, God's deliverance, and God's faithfulness.

After sending his wives, children, and everything he owned ahead of him across the Jabbok river, Jacob was left alone. Here God met with him. Jacob had first encountered God at Bethel, then at Mahanaim, and now at Peniel. At Bethel and Mahanaim, the Lord had reassured Jacob of his help, but at Peniel Jacob learned something far more. This meeting with God would drastically alter him, making him fit to enter the Promised Land.

Jacob's wrestling with the Lord at Peniel is one of the most mysterious incidents in Scripture. In many ways it is frightening, yet ultimately it reveals a beautiful, intimate, and transforming encounter with God. For Jacob, Peniel became the most sacred place where he encountered God. Though our experience could never match Jacob's, his story teaches us much about how God still deals with us today. Peniel offers many lessons about contagious blessings. Let us consider five of these contagious blessings: contagious perseverance, contagious prayer, contagious penitence, contagious power, and contagious price. I want to consider this with you from Genesis 32:22–32, especially verses 29b–30a, "And he [God] blessed him [Jacob] there. And Jacob called the name of the place Peniel."

Contagious Perseverance

Old Testament believers often gave special names to places of divine encounter with God. They did that so that when generations of children after them asked, "Why is this place called Peniel," they could answer: "This is where father Jacob had a divine encounter with God." At Peniel, Jacob tasted as never before the saving experience of personally knowing God and his blessing. Peniel means "the face of God" in Hebrew. Jacob chose the name because he could say, "I have seen God face to face, and my life is preserved" (Gen. 32:30), or more literally, "my soul has been delivered." Jacob could also have said, "I have seen God face to face, and my soul knows his salvation in the Messiah. It knows the healing, redeeming touch of his hand and heart."

Do you recall places in your life where God met with you and spoke to you through his Word in such a way that you could say, "God met with me here and blessed me in his Son"?

On the evening of his encounter with God, Jacob was alone. No doubt Jacob realized the enormity of his return to Canaan, which was the Promised Land to him and his seed. This is where the Messiah would be born one day—he would live here and perform his ministry, die, be buried, and rise again. He would be a descendant of Jacob because God had made that promise to Jacob and his ancestors. Jacob was the covenant head of the family that would give birth to Christ. So Jacob knew how important it was for him to return to Canaan. In spite of his conniving character, Jacob took time to be alone, presumably to wait, to think, to pray, and to listen to what God had to say.

Suddenly, Jacob heard someone approaching in the darkness. His heart must have beat hard as the powerful hand of a nameless assailant laid hold of him. Soon Jacob, who was no pushover, found himself locked in an intense wrestling match. We are told in verse 24, "There wrestled a man with him until the breaking of the day." This was not the sort of wrestling match we see today. This was a death-grapple.

Imagine the sweating hands of another human being grabbing your own. Imagine the pressure of another man's legs compressing yours. Imagine Jacob gasping, reeling, staggering backwards and forwards as he resisted his opponent's moves and tried to get a grip on him. Jacob put forth his utmost energy in this match, for the battle was fierce. Jacob wrestled on and on. He did not want to be strangled nor have his back broken. This fierce struggle went on for hours as Jacob labored against his assailant in the dark.

Jacob was a man of unusual physical strength. Early in his life, he had rolled away a stone from the mouth of a well which a number of shepherds were unable to move (Gen. 29:10). But he had to exert all of his enormous strength throughout the long hours of the night when he wrestled with the Angel of God.

At first, Jacob did not realize that he was wrestling with a person who looked like a human being but was really a theophany, or a manifestation of God in the form of a human. Although the Angel refused to give his name, it is clear from Hosea 12:4 that he was not just any angel. This being was none other than God the Son, or Jesus Christ, in a pre-incarnate appearance on earth. Jacob was wrestling with the God-man Messiah, who would one day descend from his own loins. That Messiah would die for Jacob's sins and rise from the dead. Jacob was wrestling with the Christ, the Creator, Judge, and Savior of the world!

The Messiah set himself against Jacob, the Bible says. Jacob did not start the wrestling match; it was not his idea. Rather, the Messiah came to Jacob and took him on. On the borders of the Promised Land, the God-man challenged Jacob, standing in his way as Jacob approached his inheritance. He wrestled with Jacob. He contended with him.

Have you ever wrestled with God in the dark? If you haven't, you probably will sometime before your life ends. You may have to wrestle against disappointment and betrayal. You may have to wrestle against pain and illness. Like others, you may have to wrestle against loss or loneliness or frustration or opposition. Some of God's finest people have wrestled against discouragement and depression. At times, they struggled with doubt. Many struggled daily against temptation, which is a strong, cunning wrestler. Like them, we may struggle against worry and anxiety. Sometimes we struggle with fear. Sometimes we face a problem for which we see no solution. We lie awake at 2:00 or 3:00 a.m. and are overwhelmed with a sense of futility or emptiness. We ask ourselves what we have achieved: nothing? We experience the dark night of the soul.

The outward circumstances of Jacob's struggle with God in human form at Peniel are unique, but the experience itself is not unusual. John Calvin writes: "All the servants of God in this world are wrestlers."

What is remarkable at Peniel is that Jacob managed to persevere all night in this wrestling match. The fighting went on, hour after hour. Wrestling matches today last only a matter of minutes but are so intense that wrestlers are totally exhausted afterward. For Jacob to wrestle the entire night is therefore astonishing. Verse 24 says, "There wrestled a man with him until the breaking of the day."

The blessing of perseverance, then, is the first contagious blessing that we see at Peniel. At some point during that long night, Jacob must have realized that his fellow-wrestler was greater than himself, and that the lesser must be blessed by the greater, as Hebrews 7:7 says. He began to sense the divine presence in his opponent. So he determined to persevere in the wrestling match, no longer just to defend himself but also to win a divine blessing from this angelic messenger of God. He cried out, "I will not let thee go, except thou bless me" (Gen. 32:26).

Contagious Prayer

Is this not a challenge for us in our own prayer lives? What do we know of wrestling with God? What do we know of clinging to him in desperation, pleading with tears through the long night of the soul as we beg him for a particular blessing?

Alexander Whyte writes, "Prayer is colossal work. Prayer takes all our heart, and all our soul, and all our strength, and all our mind, and all our life." We may pray like Jacob at Peniel when we are in a crisis.

We may pray like him when our need is unusually urgent. But must we wait for a crisis to wrestle with God to ask him for a particular blessing? How much do we need to learn about true prayer to come to the point of saying, like Jacob, "I will not let thee go, except thou bless me"?

These words of Jacob were not arrogant. They were spoken by an exhausted, helpless, broken man who would not let go of his God. It was the mark of true faith. Faith will not let go of God. God's purpose, then, in making us struggle thus is to bring us to our knees, clinging to him until we receive a blessing.

Peniel shows us the reward of persevering in prayer with Almighty God. Peniel became a place of great blessing for Jacob because it was where he struggled with God in prayer. Prayer is a prerequisite to blessing. We can talk and preach and even worship God, but until we experience a time of intense struggling with him in prayer, we will not discover a place of contagious blessing.

To find the contagious blessing of perseverance, it was necessary for Jacob to be alone. We are often so busy today that we scarcely have time to be alone. Even when we are alone, we feel we should be listening to music or a lecture or sermon. But frequent solitude is essential for an effective, wrestling prayer life. It can then become a place where we receive great blessing through the sanctifying work of the Spirit.

There are striking parallels between Jacob wrestling with the Angel of the Covenant and our wrestling with Almighty God in prayer. When you wrestle with someone, you cannot stand five feet away; you must come to grips with that person. You must take hold of your opponent as he takes hold of you. You must rigorously grapple with each other.

Similarly, in true prayer, we rigorously and intimately take hold of the Eternal God, and he of us, just as God and Jacob laid hold of each other. When did you last take hold of God in such an intense struggle? Or must Isaiah say of you: "And there is none that calleth upon thy name, that stirreth up himself to take hold of thee: for thou hast hid thy face from us, and hast consumed us, because of our iniquities" (Isa. 64:7)?

Two things helped Jacob persevere throughout that long night of wrestling: solitude and strife. He was alone and he was desperately afraid of meeting his brother Esau and his armed militia. Today, solitude and strife still characterize a believing, persevering wrestler with God. Neither is easy to endure, but the combination of both is a great asset to prayer. We utter our best prayers when we are alone and when we are gripped with fear.

The old Scottish Reformers often said, "You should pray until you pray through." By that they meant: Pray until you know that you've been in contact with God and tasted communion with him. Persevere in prayer; don't let God alone until he has blessed you.

Persevering prayer is greatly lacking in the

church today. When I was working on a doctorate in Reformation and Post-Reformation Theology at Westminster Seminary Philadelphia in the 1980s, I wondered why the Reformers and Puritans had more fruitful ministries than we generally have today, considering that the content of their sermons was not so different from ours. I finally concluded that, in addition to the sovereignty of God, the reason why their work was more blessed was that they spent so much time wrestling in prayer.

Luther, for example, spent two or three hours each day in prayer. "Meditation, temptation, and prayer make a minister," he writes. He once said to Philip Melanchthon, "I have so much to do tomorrow that I need to spend an extra hour in prayer." What happens to our prayer life when we have too much to do? Do we cut back on our prayers? Why? So often we treat prayer as an appendix to our life, whereas the Reformers treated prayer as life itself. Once, when overhearing Luther pray (he always prayed aloud to stave off Satan), Melanchthon exclaimed, "Gracious God! What faith! What Spirit! What reverence! Yet with what holy familiarity does Master Martin pray."

Consider also John Welsh, the son-in-law of the Scottish Reformer, John Knox, who prayed seven hours a day. He would seldom let a night slip by without rising early to pray. His wife, who feared Welsh would catch cold in the chilly side-rooms of a north Scotland home, would beg him to come back to bed for his health's sake. He would reply through the closed door, "Oh my dear wife, I have the souls of three thousand to answer for, and I know not how it is with many of them!" Sometimes she would hear him cry out as he wrestled with God, saying, "Lord, wilt Thou not grant me Scotland? Lord, grant me Scotland!"

I am not suggesting that you should pray seven hours a day. Yet I am convinced that you cannot be genuine wrestlers with God if you spend only a few minutes with him in private prayer each day. A life of communion eats up quality time—but there is no better time well spent on earth that this. When in her old age I asked my mother, who has been for decades one of the best prayer warriors I know, averaging two hours per day in prayer, "What would you do differently if you could live your life over again?" her immediate response was, "I'd pray more." The more we pray, generally speaking, the more we realize how little we pray and how profitable and contagious prayer is.

Let us take to heart the wise advice of Andrew Bonar: "In spite of Satan, pray; spend hours in prayer; rather neglect friends than not pray; rather fast, and lose breakfast, dinner, tea, and supper—and sleep too—than not pray. And we must not only talk about prayer; we must pray in right earnest. The Lord is near. He comes softly while the virgins slumber."

Are you truly wrestling daily with God? Like Jacob, have you sensed how contagious prayer can be in your life? Have you known the blessings of this kind of encounter with God?

Contagious Penitence

Peniel was a place of blessing because it was a place of contagious perseverance, but also because it was a place of contagious penitence. Penitence, or repentance, is inseparable from persevering prayer. It is impossible to be in the presence of God and to experience his holiness, righteousness, and majesty without being aware of our sinfulness, our need for profound humility, and that in God's sight we are guilty sinners who deserve death and hell.

Peniel reveals contagious penitence particularly through two actions of the Angel of God:

1. *The Angel's crippling touch.* When the Angel touched Jacob in the hollow of his thigh, his hip was wrenched out of its socket. That was probably when Jacob realized his opponent was no mere man. The late Scottish preacher, Douglas MacMillan, who was a wrestler in his youth, writes, "It would require a very severe blow or twist to dislocate the thigh joint of a fit man." But this angelic wrestler merely touched Jacob's thigh, and immediately the hip was pushed out of joint.

Throughout the wrestling match, the heavenly antagonist was restraining himself, limiting his actions to that of a human. But now it was daybreak, and the Angel didn't want Jacob to see him clearly.

So with a mere touch, he disabled Jacob. Jacob was broken. As MacMillan says, "Every single throw that a wrestler uses centers around the pivot of his thigh. Injure a wrestler's thigh and he is finished." If you can disable a wrestler in his thigh, you have him under control.

The Angel did not batter or crush Jacob's thigh but merely touched it. He used his divine power just enough to break Jacob's pride and self-reliance. He touched Jacob in the place where he could break him and bring him to his knees.

God still operates this way today. For example, a woman in Scotland came to her pastor and said, "God has so humbled me that I believe I could submit to anything he sends my way—well, with one exception."

"What's the exception?" asked the pastor.

She hesitated, "I couldn't accept it if he gave my husband cancer."

What do you suppose God did? That's right, her husband got cancer. And how did she do? She did just fine. God broke her through this cancer so completely that now she is completely dependent on him.

That is precisely what happened to Jacob. God touched him in his most vulnerable place so that, for the rest of his life, Jacob would be reminded of his weakness and lean on God in radical dependency. Jacob was in the grip of God's relentless, crippling grace!

Jacob was in agony when his hip went out of

joint. He knew he could never win this fight. He was a beaten man. But the amazing thing is that he wouldn't give up. He persevered in clinging to his conqueror and, in desperation, threw his arms around the one whom he could never defeat. Sensing the divine, Jacob clung more tightly than ever to the Angel of the Covenant even as the Angel clung tightly to Jacob. Why? We find the answer in verse 26, "I will not let thee go, except thou bless me."

Jacob's wrestling with the Angel included two phases. In the first phase, an Angel who looked like a man strove with Jacob and Jacob did not get the victory. In the second phase, Jacob took the initiative in the struggle and gained the victory. Here is the mighty paradox of grace. After Jacob was wounded, bruised, and broken, he then took the initiative to keep striving with God until he gained the victory. The secret of that striving was that he went on—not in his own strength, ingenuity, or scheming, but by clinging to the one who alone could help him. The secret of his victory was his own helplessness and his desperate dependence on God.

The wonderful truth that emerges from this passage is that Jacob was of more use to God as a failure who could not go forward without limping than as a self-reliant, scheming, self-justifying, self-made success. What does that teach you about some of the failures you have experienced? If you think you are all washed up because your failures have humiliated you and brought you down, consider that perhaps

God is crippling you because he couldn't move you to repentance any other way. Maybe you don't understand what happened; all you know is that you keep trying to run and you can't any longer because you hurt too much. You try to do the things you used to do in life and fail because you no longer have the strength. The confidence you had in your own ability is gone. That brokenness may be God's way to bring you back to himself, where you can cling to him, begging him for his mercy to go on.

Likewise, Jacob clung to the Angel of the Covenant, who said, "Let me go, for the day breaketh" (v. 26). Jacob's response was, "I will not let thee go, except thou bless me." He held onto the Angel because he knew his opponent was God. He clung to God because he knew that without God he could do nothing. God had won the victory in this wrestling match, but so did Jacob, for God would not let Jacob go. When Jacob was at his weakest he was at his strongest, for God's strength was made perfect in his weakness (cf. 2 Cor. 12:9). The man that God would not let go became the man who would not let God go. That is grace.

Finally, Jacob really loses and yet really wins—he wins by losing. And God wins. This is a win-win wrestling match. Jacob has power through weakness and prevails; God has power through strength and prevails. His strength is made perfect in weakness.

So there is no tie here, but a double win—that is the way of grace. Jacob wins by being blessed; God

wins by blessing, by being the Blesser and the blessing in Christ Jesus, and getting glory to himself.

Has God ever broken you down until you could
only cling to him in absolute dependence? Prayer
and repentance does not center on your own strength
and abilities or even on your weakness and inability;
it centers on the power of God that is poured into us
in our weakness and dependence on him.

The apostle Paul says it best: "When I am weak"—
weak in self—"then am I strong"—strong in Christ
(2 Cor. 12:10). Our problem today is that we depend
too much on our own strength. Until we realize how
weak we are and fall upon the sovereign wisdom and
power of God, we will not experience places of blessing in our lives, our churches, and our nation.

Jacob knew the blessing of repentance only after
he was broken by the touch of the living God. Is that
your experience as well? And having experienced
this, have you not longed to experience it again and
again? Is there not something inexpressibly contagious about the sweetness of clinging to God in
penitent dependence?

2. *Jacob's new name.* The second evidence of contagious repentance at Peniel was the new name Jacob
received after he was crippled by the Angel of the
Covenant.

In verse 27 the Angel asks Jacob, "What is thy
name?" That question may strike you as strange.

Didn't the Angel of the Covenant know Jacob's name? Why then did he ask?

Jacob had just asked for the Angel's blessing. God's way of blessing often begins with repentance, and repentance often begins with probing questions such as: "What is thy name?"

Jacob answered simply, "Jacob" (v. 27). Jacob gave his name, and in that simple response he finally came clean before God. He confessed who he was and what he had done. In saying his name, Jacob was reminded of what he had done in the past twenty years: how he cheated his brother, lied to his father, deceived Laban, and acted shamefully to his family. God asked him who he was, and he admitted, "I am Jacob, the heel-clutcher, the supplanter, the twister, the clever, devious, self-reliant, ambitious man. That is who I am."

Finally Jacob admitted who he was. Twenty years before, when asked the same question at the bedside of his old, blind, father, Isaac, Jacob had responded with a lie. Jacob had said, "Esau—Esau, thy firstborn."

God would not let Jacob enter the Promised Land as Jacob the deceiver, who had been making clever schemes, dividing up his family and his property, and preparing enormous bribes for his brother. Jacob was doing all he could to save himself from the anger of his avenging brother. At the same time, he was pouring out his fears to God in the longest prayer recorded in Genesis. So there were two sides of Jacob: one who planned with scheming, and the other who prayed to God for guidance.

God did not want Jacob to believe his clever strategies had solved his difficulties with Esau and brought him back to the Promised Land. So God struggled with Jacob, wrestling with him through the night to bring him to his knees in repentance. Jacob had always wanted God's blessing, and that was to his credit. He had tried to obtain that blessing by his own cleverness, and that was useless now. He could no longer plan or scheme or plot; he could only cling in brokenness to God. So he pleaded with God to give him what he could never get himself. In effect he begged, "Thou must bless me. I cannot do it. I have no more schemes or plans. There is no more trickery left in me."

God deals with us in a real way. He brings us to sweet, contagious repentance at those places where he blesses us. He makes us admit who we truly are before him, so that he can unveil to us what he is in Christ. How important it is, then, that we stop our scheming and self-righteousness and become nothing but a Jacob, a hell-worthy sinner before God.

God will not bless us with spiritual liberty as long as we have unconfessed sin in our lives. We will not see his face of mercy as long as we cling more to sin than to God. Isaiah 59:2 tells us, "But your iniquities have separated between you and your God, and your sins have hid his face from you, that he will not hear." Far too often, we feel distanced from God because we refuse to admit to him what we are and what we have done. But the apostle John tells us that, if we continue to deny this reality, we will defeat and destroy ourselves (1 John 1:9).

Have you ever admitted before God that you were like Jacob? Have your past sins come back to haunt you as they came back to Jacob? When Jacob gave his name, he admitted that he was nothing but a deceptive, undeserving sinner. What about you? Have you, too, admitted you were an unworthy sinner coming to the Savior for true salvation that is possible only after he changes you from within?

God's response to Jacob's penitence was, "Thy name shall be called no more Jacob, but Israel: for as a prince hast thou power with God and with men, and hast prevailed...and he blessed him there" (vv. 28, 29). Perhaps for the first time in his life, Jacob obtained a blessing clean and untarnished. He got it directly from the hand of God, not through any of his own efforts.

When you admit that, like Jacob, you are a supplanter, God will change you from within. Like Jacob, your name will be changed to Israel, for God will make you a prince. You see, the amazing twist of the gospel is that when Jacob acknowledged his real name, God gave him a better name. Oh, what a difference there is between God calling us Christians and our presuming to call ourselves Christians without just cause! The former is divine grace; the latter, self-deceit.

From an earthly perspective, Jacob was an ugly, unlovable name. Even Jacob's brother, Esau, could rightly say in Genesis 27:36, "Is not he rightly named Jacob? for he hath supplanted me these two times: he took away my birthright; and, behold, now he hath taken away my blessing."

But from God's perspective, Jacob was a temporary name, for Jacob was sovereignly and graciously loved by God from eternity past. Romans 9:11–13 says, "For the children being not yet born, neither having done any good or evil, that the purpose of God according to election might stand, not of works, but of him that calleth, it was said unto her [Rebekah], The elder shall serve the younger. As it is written, Jacob have I loved, but Esau have I hated."

Esau might be coming after Jacob with four hundred men, but God had made a covenant to protect Jacob, the unworthy supplanter, and was betrothed unto him forever (Hos. 2:9). The eternal, committed love of God was the secret of Jacob's name change, his personal transformation, and his contagiousness.

Likewise, the secret of your new birth in Christ is God's grace that leads you to repentance and to the cross of Christ. The precious Savior was willing to take upon himself your unworthy name and sin so that he could impute to you his beautiful name and perfect righteousness. In Christ alone, you then become a prince with God so you may live with contagious power.

Contagious Power

Peniel was a place of blessing because it was a place of contagious power. As God tells Jacob in verse 28, "Thy name shall be called no more Jacob, but Israel, for as a prince hast thou power with God and with men, and hast prevailed."

During the night of wrestling with the Angel of the Lord, Jacob realized that the Angel was really God who had come to him and opposed him. He was dealing with the Lord God. Jacob realized then that the greatest terror in his life was not Esau! Jacob had to have God's blessing to keep going. That blessing was more important to him than anything else. And then, as the prophet Hosea says: "Yea, he [Jacob] had power over the angel, and prevailed" (12:4). Jacob overcame the Angel, Hosea says, by weeping and "making supplication over him." Jacob came to the end of his strength; he could no longer wrestle but simply cling to the Angel as a little child clings to his parent. He overcame the Angel only after he was broken and begged for mercy.

At times, circumstances or other people prevent us from moving forward in some endeavor. Yet, in all our struggles, no matter what they are, we must deal with God. In every situation in life, our relationship with God comes first. Calvin writes: "Whenever we are tempted our business is truly with God." At first sight this seems absurd, but experience and reason teach us it is true. The problem, the struggle, the affliction, or difficulty is not the primary issue; our relationship with God matters above all. Without the blessing of God, we can do nothing.

God will not force himself upon us. The Angel of the Lord could have annihilated Jacob at any moment, but he wanted Jacob to come to the end of himself first. He wanted to break Jacob so that he would realize his need and beg for mercy from God. Likewise God comes to us in our afflictions and seemingly opposes us until we realize how powerless we are and how dependent we are on the mercy of God. He wants to break us until we say with tears, "I will not let thee go, except thou bless me."

"He, having challenged us to this contest, at the same time furnishes us with the means of resistance so that he both fights against us and for us," Calvin goes on to write. "For while he lightly opposes us, he supplies invincible strength whereby we overcome." God lightly opposes us, Calvin says. He merely puts forth his finger and we are broken. But in that touch, God also offers us invincible strength to cling to, for he is really on our side.

The name *Israel* that Jacob received from God means "God fights with you" as well as "you have fought with God." This new name also suggests the destiny of God's people, who would suffer many trials and perplexities. At times it would seem that God was against the children of Israel. But ultimately, he was on the side of his children, as he was with Jacob, now called Israel. God's power will prevail in his children so that they will prevail with him.

Jacob, now stricken by God and afflicted, was called Israel. Likewise, his descendant, the Messiah, would suffer so greatly that it would seem like God was striving against his Christ. But ultimately, God would fight in and through Christ. That is true of everyone who is united to Christ by faith. We suffer and struggle and wrestle with God, but when we are finally broken and cling to him, we become Israel, prince of God. Jesus Christ fights for us and in us. And in him we receive overcoming power in all our difficulties.

In Christ, we receive a new name and are personally transformed. In Christ, we overcome sin through the anointing of his Spirit. In Christ, we overcome our enemies. In Christ, we overcome past sins, present sins, and future sins. In Christ, "we are more than conquerors through him that loved us" (Rom. 8:37). Because of Christ, no person, no enemy, no Esau has the power "to separate us from the love of God in Christ Jesus our Lord" (Rom. 8:38–39).

The power reflected in Jacob's name change is not a physical power. It is not mental or magical or meritorious. Rather, it is the power that flows out of God's mercy through Jesus Christ and God's promises in him. Jesus Christ, the Angel of the Covenant, wrestles and prevails over all the powers of hell for all the Jacobs who his Father has given to him from eternity. He became a worm in Gethsemane, Gabbatha, and Golgotha as he took the place of sinful Jacobs like you and me to deliver us from sin. This power flows out of Jesus Christ who perfectly obeyed the Law of God on our behalf to rescue sinners like Jacob from the pit of condemnation and empower them so that they, like Israel, might be used to win others to Christ.

We exercise this contagious power in the following ways in dependence on the Spirit's grace:

1. By being so acutely aware of our weakness and sin that we lean only on Christ for our strength and salvation. We learn that when we are weak in ourselves, we are strong in Christ. As Isaiah 33:23 says, "The lame take the prey."

2. By exercising simple, childlike faith in Christ, so that we adhere to Christ's imperative: "Ye believe in God; believe also in me" (John 14:1).

3. By mightily striving for the ingathering of Christ's kingdom. Believers who wrestle for Christ may suffer violence, but they will take it in the end by power (Matt. 11:12).

4. By patterning our lives after Christ so that we can be the salt of the earth and the light of the world (Matt. 5:13–14). All the while we must pray that "by our godly conversation, others may be gained for Christ" (Heidelberg Catechism, Q. 86).

Jacob experienced that kind of persistent power at Peniel. The Angel of the Covenant blessed him, verse 29 says. Anyone who meets God and is blessed by him cannot remain unchanged. He or she will be blessed with power both with God and with man.

Today we speak far too lightly about being blessed by God. To be blessed, in the Hebraic sense of the word, involves worshiping God as he has revealed himself in his Word. It involves receiving God's goodness by faith and knowing the joy of obeying his commandments. To be blessed involves receiving, embracing, and giving. It is the transforming, progressive experience of beholding the beauty of the Lord. For example, if you are truly blessed by a sermon, the power of God will come down upon you and you will be utterly transformed. Often the process will involve such pain and suffering that you will become aware of the heinousness of your sin and be filled with profound impressions about the holy character of God. True blessing will make you fall more profoundly in love with Christ. And it will move you forward as you traverse the King's highway of holiness, longing for the day when you can be with Christ forever.

Jacob left Peniel with the power of God resting upon him. Verse 31 tells us, "As he passed over Penuel, the sun rose upon him."

Notice, first, that Israel left Peniel. He could not stay in this special place of blessing, this mountaintop of communion with God, but had to return to the road of spiritual pilgrimage.

Second, the "sun rose upon him." A sunrise is a beautiful and powerful thing. It conveys power in three ways:

- It suggests *promise*. A sunrise conveys the promise of a new day, but in Jacob's case, it was also a sign of a transformed man in a new day. The sunrise is also symbolic of the Son of righteousness rising with healing in his wings. Oh, what powerful promises Christ offers our needy souls!

- It suggests *peace*. A powerful and calm peace seems to settle in during a sunrise. Likewise, how peaceful we feel in the presence of Jesus Christ, the Prince of peace, whose blood was shed for our sins. When Christ the Son of righteousness arises in a sin-condemned soul and applies his blood to that soul, the peace that passes all understanding powerfully fills that soul.

- It suggests *purity*. When the sun rises and reaches down into valleys, it seems as if an angel from heaven has come down to wash the hills and the valleys; everything seems beautiful and clean. Likewise, when Christ Jesus rises within us, we long to bring every thought captive in obedience to our pure and delightful Savior (2 Cor. 10:5).

So Israel left Peniel, moving forward in the strength of the Son of righteousness, clothed, as it were, with a powerful promise, a powerful peace, and a powerful purity. Still today, when believers possess the wonderful benefits of the Son of righteousness, their very lives are powerfully contagious as they move forward in the strength and beauty of the Lord.

Contagious Price

After Peniel, Jacob progressed toward Canaan, the land of his inheritance, to meet his brother, Esau. He was blessed, but he was also crippled. He was in pain. As Kent Hughes writes, "The bright morning sun revealed a stooped, bleeding, bruised man in tattered clothes, dark with soil and sweat, dragging a leg and grimacing with each step" (*Genesis* [Wheaton: Crossway, 2004], 402). Verse 31 says, "He halted upon his thigh." God put a permanent mark on Jacob, and his descendants forever honored that by refusing to eat the sinew around the hip socket of animals (v. 32). Jacob paid the price of God's blessing for the rest of his life. He went into Canaan with joy, yet he was also in pain.

How can pain be contagious—so contagious that verse 32 is appended to this moving wrestling match? A true Christian learns that without pain, there is no gain. But pain and suffering can also be contagious when people see the godly fruit that flows from them. Love has a price, but the price is always worth paying. God's way with us is often the way of severe mercy,

granting us what we think we cannot bear and taking from us what we think we cannot miss. Yet when
others see that these severe mercies drive us closer to
God and make us more like Christ, they may wish to
have what we possess.

Even the world is watching us when we are in
pain. They are checking us out especially then to see
if Christianity is worth its salt.

Jacob left Peniel with a new name and a new way
of walking, inseparable parts of the package of God's
grace. The new name would forever remind him of
his destiny in Christ, and the limp would forever
remind him that God had overpowered him. His dis-
ability would remind him to the end of his earthly
life of the true source of his strength and blessing.
It would bring back thoughts about the night he was
broken and cried out to God for mercy, and then
received a blessing from God.

A century ago, some theologians believed that
Jacob's experience at Peniel referred to a kind of second blessing that every believer should ask of God.
God may, of course, give some of his people very
unusual experiences after they are born again, but it is
better to view Jacob's experience as a special fatherly
way that God deals with all of us who are believers.
He brings us to a painful crisis of some kind or brings
us into a period of intense struggle. In the process,
our self-confidence drains away. Our strength ebbs.
We learn how to rely on God rather than ourselves.
Such lessons may need to be repeated in our lives

because we are such slow learners. When Abraham's name was changed, it was changed forever. When Sarai's name was changed, it was changed forever. But Jacob would still often be referred to as Jacob. Sometimes Scripture would call him Jacob; sometimes, Israel. But, after Peniel, he would be a man on the way to blessing.

In his loving wisdom, God sometimes injures us, just as he dislocated Jacob's hip and left him limping. God may take something or someone out of our lives. He may allow something to happen that makes us feel ineffective or crippled. The touch of God during such times can seem cruel but it is in truth kind, for in it we learn to say, "Thou hast afflicted me in truth and faithfulness."

Is there some sin in your life today that God can stop only by putting your hip out of joint? No matter how sore you are, you will receive blessing and power if you submit to God's loving touch. Again and again, God has to touch us in our sore places and put things out of joint for our benefit. Of course, our flesh rebels against this. But God does what is truly best for us. He does not confer with our flesh and blood. He sanctifies spiritual pain to us so that we learn to embrace it as a blessing.

Let us pray for grace to thank God for crippling us to bring us to him. We learn more through such experiences than we do when our lives are free of trials. Paul needed a thorn in the flesh to keep him dependent on God. Ultimately he learned to thank

God for that thorn, saying, "I take pleasure in infir-
mities, in reproaches, in necessities, in persecutions,
in distresses for Christ's sake: for when I am weak,
then am I strong" (2 Cor. 12:10).

No doubt some of you are wrestling in the dark.
If so, this passage says to you, "Cling to God, and his
blessing will certainly begin." You may go on your
way limping, but this passage assures you that God's
touch is deliberate.

After a night of darkness, a new day dawned for
the weary, broken, limping Jacob. It was a day of
blessing and a day of grace. And Jacob's response to
that promise was to call the name of the place Peniel: "for I have seen God face to face, and my life is
preserved."

As believers our lives are saved, not because we
have seen God face to face, but because we have seen
him face to face in Christ Jesus. The glory of God is
in the face of Christ. We no longer need to ask, like
Jacob, "Tell me thy name," for we already know the
name of our blessed Savior, Jesus Christ. It is the
name above every name, and it is the source of our
confidence.

Despite his limp, Jacob made progress in his pilgrimage back to Canaan. He was "halting upon his
thigh," but he was still moving forward. God was
healing Jacob. The wonder of God's touch is that he
not only wounds and breaks us, but he also heals us.

Isn't that the experience of every believer? The
Holy Spirit breaks us down, unveils our sin, brings

us to repentance, empties us and wounds us—all to lead us to Christ and to spiritually heal us. Though we will limp to the end of life's journey, God will send us walking, running, even leaping along the way, like "calves of the stall" (Mal. 4:2). He fulfils what Hosea 6:1 says: "Come, and let us return unto the LORD: for he hath torn, and he will heal us; he hath smitten, and he will bind us up." This, too, is contagious.

Wounding, Healing, Marking

God left his mark on Jacob. That mark left such a profound effect on Israel that the children of Israel would not eat from the hip socket area for centuries—at least until the time of Moses who authored Genesis 32:32. God's mark on Jacob became a contagious blessing for Israel.

If God doesn't leave his mark on you, you will not be blessed with lasting profit from your afflictions. We must learn to welcome both pain and progress in our walk with God, realizing that we learn more through affliction than prosperity. Both are part of the contagious price of God, for he is most worthy to fit us for service in this life and the life to come. Let us then ask ourselves as we walk forward in God's grace:

- Despite my inconsistencies, is the persevering character of my spiritual life contagious? Despite the inadequacy of my prayers, is my prayer life contagious? Despite my imperfections, is my life contagiously penitent? Despite my weaknesses, does my life convey contagious power? Despite my complaints, am I willing to suffer pain for the contagious freedom I find in Christ?

- Do I realize that my profession of faith will be powerless if it does not ring true in my daily life? My words and actions will not be contagious. When I look back, isn't it true that the Christians who made the deepest impression on me were those in whom I could see perseverance, prayer, penitence, power, and price?

- Am I praying for grace that God will mark me with his blessing in every trial, every place of communion with himself, and every place of weakness? Those places are what marked Jacob's blessings as the work of God. May God make my life an open and written epistle of the grace of God in Jesus Christ, so that I may be both blessed and a blessing.

- Am I thanking God that he has only touched me in the thigh? Why doesn't he destroy that thigh? Why does he touch only one thigh and not both of them? Why doesn't he put all the bones of my body out of joint? The answer is: he did that to Christ instead of me. Therefore my suffering Savior cried out, "I am poured out like water, and all my bones are out of joint: my heart is like wax; it is melted in the midst of my bowels" (Ps. 22:14).

For Christ's sake, God tailor-makes our afflictions. Each one fits our shoulders perfectly. Do we realize that we have needed every affliction we have ever received?

- What is my name before God? Am I, like Jacob, still trying to manipulate my own life and make my own arrangements? Am I still resisting God's will? If God can save crafty Jacob, why don't I plead with him to save me? Lord, break me so that the God of Jacob becomes my God and blesses me with his blessing.

More than twenty times in Scripture, God calls himself "the God of Jacob." His love for Jacob and of the glory of Jacob flows through his Word. "Happy is he that hath the God of Jacob for his help…yea, happy is that people, whose God is the LORD," says Psalm 144:15. Let the grace of God for unworthy sinners move you to ask, seek, and knock at God's throne for the grace Jacob experienced at Peniel.

4

Consistent Integrity

Daniel (Daniel 1)

Along life's journey, we sometimes come to a cross-roads where we could turn in different directions. We face our biggest crossroads of all, perhaps, when we are teenagers. Will I go to college or find a job? Will I study medicine or history? Will I become a chef, an electrician, a computer tech? Will I enter the military? How soon will I marry? Each of these questions is part of the larger question: "How will I spend the rest of my life?"

Recently, I asked a fifty-year-old man next to me on an airplane how he would spend the rest of his life. He said he had just retired and planned to spend the rest of his life golfing in Florida. When I asked more questions, he admitted that golfing wasn't really an exciting or useful way to spend the rest of his life.

This morning, I beg you all—especially you, dear young people—not to waste your life. The possibilities ahead of you are almost endless, but be careful. Most of them can waste your life. We live in a broken world surrounded by people—including many who claim to be Christian—who do nothing more than waste their time, their energy, their resources, their lives. Imagine the glory God would receive if all of you young people did not follow the ways of the world, but instead, by God's grace, chose to live for his glory. Imagine how appealing and contagious your lives would be if you determined to follow God with consistent integrity.

But what exactly is integrity, you ask. Good question. We often talk about how much society needs it, but I'm afraid that we seldom bother to define and understand it. Stephen Carter, author of a book on integrity, says that "integrity is like the weather: everybody talks about it but nobody knows what to do about it. Integrity is that stuff we always say we want more of. We want our elected representatives to have it. We want it in our spouses, our children, our friends. We want it in our schools and our houses of worship." ("Becoming People of Integrity," *Christian Century,* March 13, 1996, p. 297).

A person of integrity lives uprightly, morally, and spiritually. The word *integrity* derives from the Latin root, *integer,* which conveys the idea of a sense of wholeness or completeness. A person of integrity steadfastly adheres to a moral or ethical code—in the case of a Christian, to God's standards as revealed in his Word. In Christ, by Christ, and for Christ's sake, he strives to consistently do what is right in God's sight. He is honest and sincere, abhorring hypocrisy and duplicity. A person of integrity discerns between right and wrong, and acts out that concern openly and transparently, even if it involves personal cost. A contagious Christian, then, is someone who strives consistently to live in whole obedience to God no matter what the price.

In his classic, *The Christian's Daily Walk,* Henry Scudder says that Christian integrity or uprightness "is a saving grace of the Holy Ghost, wrought in the heart of a man rightly informed in the knowledge of God in Christ, whereby his soul stands so entirely and sincerely right towards God, that in the true disposition, bent, and firm determination of his will, he would, in every faculty and power of soul and body, approve himself to be such an one as God would have him to be, and would do whatsoever God would have him to do, and all as God would have him, and that for and unto God, and his glory" (*The Christian's Daily Walk* [Harrisonburg, Va.: Sprinkle, 1984], 155).

A Christian of integrity realizes that the living God, who is himself a perfect God of upright integrity, has a claim on all our possessions; our mind, soul, and strength; our gifts and talents; our use of time; our friendships; our entire being. A Christian of integrity prays, "Let integrity and uprightness preserve me" (Ps. 25:21).

That is how Daniel lived. Let us consider his life of consistent integrity, limiting ourselves to Daniel 1, particularly highlighting verses 8, 14, and 21: "But Daniel purposed in his heart that he would not defile himself with the portion of the king's meat, nor with the wine which he drank: therefore he requested of the prince of the eunuchs that he might not defile himself.... So he [Melzar] consented to them in this matter, and proved them ten days.... And Daniel continued even unto the first year of king Cyrus."

Let us examine Daniel's integrity, first, in his resolution (v. 8); second, in his trial (v. 14); and third, in his perseverance (v. 21).

Daniel's Resolution

The opening words of the book of Daniel are worth pausing over. We read, "In the third year of the reign of Jehoiakim king of Judah came Nebuchadnezzar king of Babylon unto Jerusalem, and besieged it. And the Lord gave Jehoiakim king of Judah into his hand, with part of the vessels of the house of God: which he carried into the land of Shinar to the house of his god; and he brought the vessels into the treasure house of his god" (Dan. 1:1–2).

This is monumental! In a few short sentences we are told that the people of God who remained in Jerusalem have been taken captive by a foreign army, and the temple of God has been plundered by Gentiles. What does that say about God's plan for his chosen people? Does he no longer care about what is happening to them? Everything is going wrong: the holy city is besieged, nearly everyone has been captured and enslaved, and the temple of God is defiled.

Imagine for a moment that you were Daniel. Foreign armies marched down your streets as you and your friends and family are carried off as slaves to a foreign country. Everything you valued has been stripped from you. Your nation's prized national symbols have been smashed and your cities left in ruins. You keep expecting to wake up from this horrific nightmare, but you never do; this is reality.

After your capture, you and thousands of other Jews were marched away from Israel across the desert to the great city of Babylon. The familiar Jordan river was far behind you; ahead were the unfamiliar waters of the Tigris and Euphrates rivers. Gone were the comforting walls of Jerusalem; in their place were the threatening and massive walls of Babylon. The empty temples of Yahweh lay broken across the wasteland, its treasures deposited in the temple of Marduk in Babylon.

Soon after arriving in Babylon, you and your friends were enrolled in an intense program of indoctrination, in which you learned the ways of Babylonian culture, religion, and politics. Babylon was the capital of the vast kingdom over which Nebuchadnezzar reigned. Babylon had walls as high as towers, upon which four chariots could ride side by side. Inside those walls, the city was lush with luxury. Its hanging gardens, supported by pillars around the metropolis, were known as one of the wonders of the world. Babylon was rich and glittering.

But Babylon was also a sinkhole of sin, a worldly city full of pride, lust, and temptation. You and your friends were brought to the two most magnificent buildings in the heart of Babylon: the king's palace and the temple of Bel, a supreme god of Babylon. According to the king's command, courtiers were assigned to you and other young men taken from a variety of conquered countries. After three years of re-education, you and the other captives were expected to be transformed into Babylonians in mind, heart, and behavior.

You were confronted with a whole new way of life. You had to learn the Babylonian language, wear Babylonian clothing, and eat Babylonian food that had been consecrated to Babylonian idols. You were immersed in Babylonian religion, literature, mythology, history, philosophy, drama, music, superstition, and astrology. Even your name was changed. Daniel, which means, "God is my judge," was changed to Belteshazzar, which means "keeper of the hid treasures of Bel."

Everywhere you went, the subliminal message was: Become a Babylonian. Forget your God. Conform. This is the only way for you. Babylon will promote you, make you rich, give you happiness and honor.

How could you resist such pressure, especially after Marduk, Babylon's god, had apparently defeated Yahweh, the God of Israel? Why should you hang on to the religion of your fathers when the temple was in ruins and the people of Israel and Judah were scattered? You could never hope to get back to your old friends in Jerusalem because that city was in ruins.

You might as well build a new life in Babylon. People in authority had given you a new name; why not assume the identity that went with it? Other captives could hang their harps in a tree and weep, but that wouldn't do them—or you—any good. Why not make the best of the situation and allow the Babylonians to benevolently brainwash you into forgetting the past and joining them for the future?

Daniel might have been tempted by such thoughts, but verse 8 tells us he did not submit to them. Rather, he resolved not to defile himself. How could Daniel still have faith in God when everything had gone so terribly wrong? Clearly, God was sustaining him. Verse 9, as we'll see shortly, makes it clear that God was at work in this situation.

Have you ever been in circumstances similar to what Daniel experienced? Have you ever felt that others were conspiring to lure you away from God's people and destroy your faith in God? Have they tried to convince you that you could not succeed in business or education or relationships without succumbing to the ways of people around you? Of course you have. Babylon, the symbol of worldliness for thousands of years, finds a kindred spirit in the worldly influences and pressures that still hound us today.

Worldliness, ultimately, is living without God. People who are worldly are controlled by the pursuits of pleasure, profit, and position. They yield to the spirit of self-seeking and self-indulgence without regard for God. The goal of worldly people is to move forward rather than upward, to live horizontally rather than vertically. They seek outward riches rather than the riches of inward holiness. That is the spirit of the world we live in today.

We live in a post-Babylonian world, but it is still an anti-God, brainwashing world. Worldly language abounds in our day. Secular, pragmatic, atheistic humanism and new age post-modernism are rampant. Materialism feeds the quest for pleasure and gratification. Entertainment seduces the hearts and minds of young people, leading them to abandon a quiet, God-fearing life as they embrace the noisy world of rock music, violent or pornographic movies, and ungodly literature. They fall prey to the idolization of sports heroes and actors and succumb to the wearing of immodest clothing. They are seduced by sexuality and premarital sex as well as aberrant forms of sexuality patently condemned in the Scriptures; like unbelievers around them, they believe that fornication and adultery are okay provided the partners mutually agree. Educators undermine faith in God and set man up as the epitome of truth.

Morality is dropping to an all-time low as pride and self-promotion are promoted as virtues rather than vices. The lusts of the flesh, of the eyes, and of the pride of life are encouraged. Violence overwhelms civility. Abortion and euthanasia are winked at. Politicians appear more concerned about reelection than spiritual, moral, and fiscal responsibility. National debt heaps up with no accountability. Anyone in authority is questioned, repudiated, and sued.

Our multi-ethnic, multi-cultural, and multi-faith society promotes a self-righteous disdain and intolerance for Christians. In a particularly subtle and dangerous way, the media seek to wipe out God from human consciousness by portraying him as a crutch for helpless, ignorant people. Not long ago, I tried to evangelize a young European while flying over Europe. He looked at me in amazement, and said, "You are the first Christian under seventy who has ever tried to convert me. I thought Christianity was only for old people." The media has brainwashed our world against Christianity in every sphere of our lives, from sports to religion. It does not let up for a minute. It uses clever propaganda, mixes lies with truth, and packages lies in beauty. Poison is mixed with the good so that we will swallow it more easily.

Truly, we live in a world where lazy opinions will not stand the test and where half-hearted Christianity will crumble. In the midst of all, the good news is that believers have been facing the temptation of worldly influences for centuries and, in many cases, God's power has been revealed. He does not always work the way we expect, but he is always faithful to those who strive, for Christ's sake, to walk with him in consistent integrity, as Daniel did.

Still, if you had just been carried away from your country to Babylon and you wanted to remain faithful to God, would you quibble about something so insignificant as food? Shouldn't you choose bigger battles to fight? Wasn't Daniel nitpicking when he refused to eat the food that was specially prepared for him and his friends?

By the end of this chapter, Daniel and his friends would be selected as the best in their class and would find themselves appointed as important advisers to the king of the Babylonian empire. For years, Daniel would rule over a wicked, murderous, and idolatrous empire. Yet how could he expect to do that if he balked at every little thing that he found offensive?

Daniel obviously had a very clear view of living in the world while not being of the world. His protestation here in chapter 1 shows us how carefully he guarded his purity before God. His years of faithful service to the Babylonian empire would also reveal how consistently he would follow God while rendering faithful service to the authorities God had placed over him. Daniel's life has some important lessons to teach us. If we are going to live contagious Christian lives in a secular world, we must learn to react like Daniel to the worldliness and evil all around us.

Resisting Temptation

The first lesson we learn from Daniel is how to resist temptation and remain undefiled in a world that is intent on tempting and defiling us.

Daniel resisted eating food offered to false gods. It was something he simply would not do. The problem was that he was in a place that only served that kind of food. The difficulties of procuring other food were immensely difficult and the temptation to simply give up and eat the food of idols was increasingly attractive. After all, Daniel was a prisoner; did he really think he could order whatever he wanted?

Some might have argued with Daniel, saying, "Be realistic, Daniel. There will be other battles to fight—just go along with this. You cannot do anything about it, anyway."

Do you recognize these temptations? They don't always seem like temptations. Often it seems more like wisdom or propriety to suggest, "It just wouldn't be proper to object right now. You can do that better at a later time." But Daniel was convinced that it would not be wise to give up now so that he might battle with temptation later. He determined that he would not defile himself with the king's food.

Do you understand the kind of pressure Daniel experienced? When in school or at work, do you easily go along with what others do, even when you know it is wrong? Do you pray for strength to reject sin? We are confronted every day with the temptation of mixing Christianity and worldliness, Babylon with Jerusalem, and keeping a form of religion but doing away with a separate and godly lifestyle.

We are also tempted to live a mixed lifestyle which says yes to the church and yes to the world. How few of us realize that when we say yes to the world, we are really saying no to God. God does not approve of half-hearted Christians.

What an easy life Daniel could have had if he had been willing to compromise! He could have kept his own religion private, couldn't he? All he had to do was go with the flow and not take things like diet so seriously. By grace, however, Daniel could not compromise. The fear of the Lord was planted in his young heart. He could not be at home in the world. He could not say yes to the world.

Daniel 1:8 tells us, "Daniel purposed in his heart that he would not defile himself with the portion of the king's meat, nor with the wine which he drank." Daniel made the decision not to eat the king's food, not because of his parents, church, or any person, but because it was the desire of his heart. He did not act out of legalism. He did not act in fear of God's punishment. He acted out of love for the Lord who was so worthy to be feared.

In addition to love, there were other important reasons why Daniel determined not to defile himself with the food of the king. First, this food failed to meet the Old Testament dietary restrictions God had established for his people, including rules for cleanliness (Lev. 7:23–27; 11:1–47; Deut. 12:15–28). Second, Daniel could not eat what was offered in the name of other gods because God had forbidden the Jews from participating in any forms of idolatry (Ex. 20:4–5; cf. Lev. 19:4; Deut. 5:7–8). Third, Daniel was motivated by jealousy—jealousy for the Lord's name and honor, which would be compromised by eating food offered to idol gods; and jealousy over his own heart, for he knew the power of temptation, of the world, and of Satan. He knew how quickly his conscience could be dulled, how prayer could suffer, and how communion with God could be broken. He therefore drew a line in the sand, purposing "in his heart" not to eat the food of the king.

Daniel's whole desire was to walk before the Lord and to live to his honor and glory. He knew from experience that "man shall not live by bread alone but by every word that proceedeth out of the mouth of God" (Matt. 4:4). He lived by faith in hope of the fulfillment of the promise of the coming Messiah.

Can you, like Daniel, say from the heart that you must flee the world and all of its temptations? Is the divine pressure of God's Word weightier for you than the peer pressure of your friends? Or do you regularly cave in to such temptation? Are you like a fish without a backbone that just drifts along with the tide? Do you act out of conviction, remaining true to God in every circumstance, or do you, like a chameleon that changes color to match its surroundings, blend in with the ways of everyone around you? Do you hide your Christianity, or do you dare to stand firm against worldly temptations?

If you are uncertain of your strength to withstand the temptation of peer pressure, here are some ways to help you through such times:

1. *Understand the strength of temptation.* Avoid

friends and places that you know will present a temptation. Remember, retreat is not defeat.

2. Search, know, love, and live the Scriptures. The Bible repeatedly teaches us how to fight temptation. Read Matthew 4 to see how Jesus fought off temptation using the Word of God.

3. Lean hard on Christ. In Christ we find the strength to resist every tempting enemy. Remember that, though Satan is mighty as a fallen angel, Christ is almighty as the living Lord.

4. Be true to God. Pray for the Holy Spirit's strength to walk in the way of God's commandments. What God thinks means more than what man thinks. Let God be big and man be small in your eyes. Let the fear of God prevail over the fear of peers. If you fear God, you need fear no one else.

5. Be true to your biblical convictions. Give of yourself in God-honoring ways in friendships, but do not give up yourself for friendship. The former demands self-sacrifice; the latter, sacrificing your inner convictions and moral principles.

6. Remember, true friends seek your best welfare. If a group of friends want to lead you from God and away from holiness, seek other friends. Remember, a true friend will lead you away from sin, not into it.

7. Take the long-term perspective. Many people reap lifelong sorrow for actions they took when friends tempted them to engage in a few sinful moments of fun. Remember that long-term happiness means more than short-term pleasure.

8. Lead rather than be led. Be a positive influence rather than being led by negative influences. A true friend exerts pressure that is positive in nature.

9. Remember that service is greater than selfishness. When he was nineteen, my brother told me, "I have discovered what life is all about and I can put it in one word."

"What's the word?" I asked.

"*Service,*" he said. "If God created us to serve him and our neighbor, so long as we serve ourselves we will be unhappy. When we serve God and our neighbor, we will be truly happy because we will be living for the purpose for which God created us."

10. Remember, inner thoughts often contradict outer actions. The words and actions of people in a group are often considerably different from what they believe in private. If you stand up for God, the very people who boldly criticize you in public may come to you in private, asking for advice when they are in trouble.

By grace, Daniel was more afraid of the snares of the devil and the pollution of sin than of losing his own life. He would rather die than sin. That is not legalism. That is not being righteous overmuch. Rather, it is love, God-given love, that returns to the God who gave it.

Daniel had the courage to say no to sin because of

the gracious influence of the Lord Jesus Christ who purposed in his heart from eternity to say no to sin during his entire life on earth. Jesus gave his life to die on the cross on behalf of all the Daniels who were enemies of God but were made to fear and love his name. May the Lord make us jealous of such Daniels. Let us pray for grace to reject the world's selfish lifestyles and to seek first the kingdom of God and its righteousness.

With such God-glorifying motives, we would be quick to think of Daniel, "The Lord will rush to make everything work out for him. Now everything will go easy for him." But no. The biggest trial was yet to come. Let us go on to that trial.

Enduring the Trial

If your friend claims that he can bounce a football on his head for ten minutes, you will toss him the ball to see if he really can. You will test his claim. Likewise, when you claim there is one God, Creator of the universe, the Father of Jesus Christ, and that you live in obedience to him, you will be tested. People will throw you the ball to see what you will do. If nobody can tell that you are a Christian, they certainly will not be drawn to Christ by your conduct. A contagious Christian life is a visibly Christian life. If they can tell, they will test you. Likewise, Daniel would now be tested by God and by man.

Daniel had purposed in his heart not to defile himself, so he took action. He approached his superior, Ashpenaz, to tell him what he had purposed in his heart (v. 8b). This action could have had so many consequences. Daniel could have been killed for such insubordination. He could have been marked forever as a troublemaker. He could have been mocked by others.

None of that happened. God had already been at work. Look at verse 9: "Now God had brought Daniel into favour and tender love with the prince of the eunuchs." God had gone before Daniel by impressing the prince with Daniel's behavior. He was already making things well. It seems he was already paving the way for Daniel to live out his convictions.

So, then, Ashpenaz's response to Daniel was a grave disappointment, for he said, "I fear my lord the king, who hath appointed your meat and your drink: for why should he see your faces worse liking than the children which are of your sort? then shall ye make me endanger my head to the king" (v. 10).

What a trial! Had not Daniel's request been a matter of prayer? Was he not motivated by a sincere desire to avoid sin? Had not God himself helped Daniel by bringing him into favor with Ashpenaz? Yet now Daniel's rejection of the spirit of the world seemed to be rejected by the Lord. What now? Should Daniel give up? Our fleshly nature would be prone to say: "Now I can fully indulge; otherwise, God would have changed the mind of the prince. I must have been too strict, too religious, too narrow-minded, too intolerant."

Satan may have planted seeds of doubt within Daniel, whispering in his ear, "Daniel, it was all only pride, stubbornness, and legalism. The Lord was not in this decision to refuse the king's food. It was only you. You are in Babylon now. Here the God of Israel will not answer your prayers. Here you must compromise with the gods and customs of Babylon."

Are you familiar with such inner doubts? You can believe that Daniel, the young man of prayer, was brought back to the feet of God in prayer through such disappointment. He must have cried out, "Lord, why? Oh God, did I not beg of thee not to let me go my own way? Now what should I do? Lord, show me thy will before I succumb to unbelief. Grant me unhindered persistence."

God did grace Daniel with perseverance. God led Daniel to try again, this time by speaking to the prince's subordinate, Melzar, who presumably would not be as afraid of Nebuchadnezzar since he did not report directly to the king. As verses 11–13 tell us, "Then said Daniel to Melzar,…prove thy servants I beseech thee, ten days; and let them give us pulse to eat, and water to drink. Then let our countenances be looked upon before thee, and the countenance of the children that eat of the portion of the king's meat: and as thou seest, deal with thy servants."

Happily, Melzar did not refuse Daniel's request. The Lord showed his favor and power in prospering this new plan that Daniel proposed, for Melzar consented to it. No doubt Daniel was so happy at that moment that he forgot about the ten-day trial he was about to enter. He and his friends still needed to prove within the next ten days that eating vegetables and water would make them healthier than eating the king's food.

Now the more difficult trial of waiting had begun. What would happen during that time of testing? Would the Lord bless the decision of Daniel and his friends to reject the king's food? Would they be killed if they did not appear healthier than the others after ten days?

God's people often experience times of waiting. Those times can be especially difficult when we do not see any signs of God's blessing. When we first receive God's promises by faith, those promises are unspeakably precious to us, but as we experience times of waiting, those promises may so test us that they seem more of a burden than a joy.

Daniel and his friends had to wait ten days to prove that God would honor their decision to eat vegetables rather than the king's meat. This was no accident; his ten-day trial was a type of the trials that believers often encounter on the pathway to heaven. Trials are removed when God reaches his perfect purposes for them, but not before. Sometimes a ten-day trial lasts for only minutes or hours; at other times, it lasts years or even the rest of a believer's life.

The Lord makes no mistakes. His trials are always perfect in time and quantity to serve his eternal and blessed purposes. Through them, all children of God are brought to the blessed place where they must die to themselves and their own righteousness. We must come to that place in our trials where we would consider the Lord righteous and just even if he did not answer our prayers the way we asked. Then we, like Daniel, could only confess, "Lord, I am unworthy that thou shouldst make a difference where there is no difference between myself and the worst of all the Babylonians in Satan's service!"

No doubt Daniel came to truly learn the meaning of his name during those ten days. Daniel means "God is my judge." He learned that man (think of Ashpenaz) and self could not be trusted. Hoping against hope, he cast himself and his trial upon the Lord, recognizing that the Lord was free to judge both his case and himself and to do with Daniel what he desired.

Dear friend, this dying to self, this surrender to God and his will, is both trying and sweet. In it, we are taught not to rely upon self. Everything comes to a standstill, and nothing remains but to sigh, "Lord, remember me in thy mercy; I am unworthy; if I perish, I perish, but then I will perish in prayer to thee. I will not let thee go."

How many times Daniel and his three friends, Shadrach, Meshech, and Abednego, must have prayed together during those ten days! There is little doubt that they often encouraged and admonished each other to persevere in obedience, no matter what Ashpenaz, Melzar, or any courtier said. But even reliance upon fellow Christians eventually falls away and we are forced to say that only the Lord can help, for the Lord alone is sovereign. In the end, the battle was between the Lord and Daniel—and then, ultimately, only between the Lord and his Son, Jesus Christ, as Daniel stood aside. Daniel himself was the Lord's case.

The Lord proved faithful, for in the final analysis, the Lord himself was being tried. Daniel 1 is really about the God of Israel gaining the victory over the gods of Babylon. Daniel was his child, and the heavenly Father will never disappoint his own. So Daniel 1:15–16 says, "At the end of ten days their countenances appeared fairer and fatter in flesh than all the children which did eat the portion of the king's meat. Thus Melzar took away the portion of their meat, and the wine that they should drink; and gave them pulse."

The Lord miraculously made a clear distinction between Daniel and his friends, proving them "fairer and fatter in flesh," or healthier, than the young men who ate the king's meat. Spiritually, God deals with us the same way. He gives his people food to eat that strengthens them in ways that the world cannot know or understand. Ten days of spiritual food will do more for the spiritual beauty and strength of believers than the world can ever offer. When we do not feast on the Lord's food, we often become lean and unhealthy. It is our own fault.

The Lord blessed Daniel and his friends for refusing the king's food, for it is God who plants faith in us, gives us strength to walk in him, tries our faith, and fulfills his promises such as 1 John 5:4: "For whatsoever is born of God overcometh the world: and this is the victory that overcometh the world, even our faith." In subsequent years, Daniel and his three friends were often tried—think only of the burning fiery furnace in chapter 3 and the den of lions in chapter 6—but God brought blessings and privileges even out of such trials. Integrity will be challenged and will suffer persecution, but in the end, it will reap righteousness and reward. Integrity will produce human detractors, but it will serve God's glory, which is far greater.

Daniel's life was not easy, but it was blessed. Let us pray for his kind of uncompromising obedience. Pray for a life that remains separate from worldly influences, not only in temptation, but also through trial. In trial we need grace to refrain from worldly ways. Moses chose to "suffer affliction with the people of God," rather than "to enjoy the pleasures of sin for a season" (Heb. 11:25). May the Lord grant you the grace to choose wisely.

God does not promise us an easy life, but he does promise us a blessed life. He also promises to prove to us in all our trials the truth of Romans 8:28: "All things work together for good to them that love God, to them who are the called according to his purpose."

As the Lord wages war against your natural, fleshly inclinations, remember that he does this to teach you the great blessedness of serving him. Everything worldly is vanity and temporary while everything that is of the Lord is invaluable and will endure forever. As Psalm 144:15 says, "Happy is that people, that is in such a case: yea, happy is that people, whose God is the LORD."

Daniel's Perseverance

The closing verse of Daniel 1 says, "Daniel continued even unto the first year of King Cyrus" (v. 21). King Cyrus began reigning in 539 B.C., nearly seventy years after Daniel was first taken captive. And during all that time, Daniel continued to live in holiness, separate from Babylonian worldliness. Even in his exalted position as the king's counselor, Daniel continued to serve God. Though other Babylonian leaders were jealous of his position, Daniel persevered. He stayed in office during the sanity and insanity of one king and the murder of three successors. For seventy long years, Daniel walked by faith in a foreign land, second only to the king in authority. He continued to trust the King of kings, believing, obeying, and knowing that he who gave the commandment to remain separate would also supply the grace to do so. By grace, he took to heart the words: "He shall never suffer the righteous to be moved" (Ps. 55:22b).

Do you ever wonder if this great prophet who dared to stand alone regretted his choice to live holy in an unholy land? The answer is, of course, no. But the deeper question must be asked: Are you following his example?

Sometimes a person who lives to be more than one hundred is asked by a reporter what the secret is of living so long. Usually the answers given are quite foolish. For example, when a 107-year-old man was asked if he ever thought about death, he responded, "No. I have a brother who is 112."

If you could have asked Daniel what the secret was of becoming nearly ninety years old while walking a God-fearing life in the midst of a heathen country, he would have had a much different answer. He would have said that it is due totally to God's grace—his pure, sovereign grace. Daniel continued to live holy before God because of God's grace. Grace is God's unmerited—yes, demerited—favor to unworthy sinners, granted for Christ's sake. The acronym GRACE teaches us:

> God's
> Riches
> At
> Christ's
> Expense

Grace was the secret of Daniel's long life of service from beginning to end. Preventing grace kept him from falling into temptation, accompanying grace brought him safely and profitably through trials, and following grace pursued him all the days of his life (Ps. 23:6). For more than seventy years, Daniel experienced God's comforting promise: "My grace is sufficient for thee" (2 Cor. 12:9). Grace is what creates and sustains contagious Christians. It is never due to anything they do. They do not strive to be contagious; they strive to be faithful, and God's grace makes them contagious.

The gracious, eternal love of a Triune God meant everything to Daniel. He tasted the drawing love of the Father who chose him from eternity. This eternal love enabled Jesus to say of Daniel and other faithful followers: "No man is able to pluck them out of my Father's hand" (John 10:29).But Daniel also experienced the sustaining love of the Son, who himself lived in perfect integrity and hence was the secret of Daniel's integrity, and who also "ever liveth to make intercession for us" (Heb. 7:25). He was also intimately acquainted with the eternal Spirit, who enables believers to sing by faith during times of trial:

> Lord, though I walk 'mid troubles sore,
> Thou wilt restore my faltering spirit;
> Though angry foes my soul alarm,
> Thy mighty arm will save and cheer it.
> Yea, thou wilt finish perfectly
> What thou for me hast undertaken;
> May not thy works, in mercy wrought,
> E'er come to naught, or be forsaken.
>
> —Psalter 429:4

Daniel never would have said, "I am a man of consistent integrity because of my religion." He was a man of consistent integrity as the fruit of the merits of his Savior who walked with perfect integrity before his Father in heaven.

Daniel continued to be faithful solely because of the Triune Jehovah, who is the great I AM THAT I AM, who abides eternally the same. Because of the great I AM, the burning bush that Moses saw burned with fire but was not consumed. As Father, God had already lit the burning bush of salvation from eternity in the Counsel of Peace. The Son fulfilled all the requirements of salvation for the hell-worthy by perfectly obeying God's Law and by enduring the agonies of death, all the while burning with love for his Father and his people. The Holy Spirit worked to save the elect, thereby guaranteeing that there would be a church that lasted until the end of the world.

Daniel did not persevere in a God-fearing lifestyle by his own efforts or of his own free will. If, as branches of the living Vine, believers had to be the fuel upon which the flame depended, the living church would have been consumed long ago. The tender branches would have withered and died from the heat of God's wrath. But the Lord Jesus Christ took all the heat of God's wrath, of hellish powers, and of the sins of his own upon himself so that his church could walk through the fire and not have a hair of her head singed. Christ walks with his people in the midst of all their fiery furnaces.

So Daniel continued to walk with God because the Triune God continued to walk with Daniel. Jehovah is the Unchangeable One. As Malachi 3:6 says, "I am the LORD, I change not; therefore ye sons of Jacob are not consumed."

Keep saying to yourself, all my perseverance flows from God's fountain of grace. It is all God's gift to me. You see, God's giving is behind all Daniel's blessings in this chapter. Verse 2 says that the Lord *gave* Jehoiakim into Nebuchadnezzar's hand. That was a judicial giving. Into Nebuchadnezzar's hands, the Lord even gave the sacred vessels from Israel's own temple. By extension, the Lord gave even the exile to Babylon and its afflictions, all to pave the way to prove that the Lord himself was mightier than the gods of Babylon. In verse 9, the verb, *to give,* resurfaces but is translated as *brought.* Literally, the Lord gave Daniel into the favor of the prince of the eunuchs. What a contrast between the gift of Daniel and the gift of Jehoiakim, but all would serve to the vindication of God's name. Then, in verse 17, we read once more that God *gave*—he gave Daniel and his friends "knowledge and skill in all learning and wisdom." You see, God is in control of every detail. He is superintending the whole process of Daniel's life and the entire history of both Israel and Babylon. God is on his throne, even if exiled Israel could not see it. Jehovah is mightier than Marduk! Therefore Daniel must persevere, for God's consistent integrity stands behind Daniel's. That's why, in some ways, Daniel 1 is more about God than Daniel.

God stays with believers because that care is inseparable from his name, cause, and glory. Oh, what comfort for believers who, like Daniel, must live through trials and persecution! No matter how hot the fiery furnace of Nebuchadnezzar and no matter how dangerous the den of lions may be, the Lord will keep his people safe.

That was not always easy for Daniel to believe. No doubt there were times when Daniel cried to the Lord, "Shall I ever continue to the end with all these temptations around and within me? Oh, Lord, I have forfeited everything so that thou wouldst be with me, but continue with me, though I have made myself unworthy a thousand times."

God sustained Daniel through the fiery furnace and the pit of lions and long afterward. God was so good to Daniel that he lived to see the days when God's promises to his people were fulfilled. When King Cyrus conquered Babylon, he allowed Daniel's people to return to Jerusalem. And Daniel lived to see that.

If you want to live a contagious life, Daniel 1 offers some important lessons about living a contagious Christian life of obedience and integrity:

- Ask for grace to examine your own level of integrity by interrogating yourself like this: Am I seeking first of all God's kingdom and his righteousness? Do I respect all of God's will and long to do it? Do I abhor hypocrisy and duplicity? Do I compromise God's Word and truth for my own expediency? Do I consistently want to please God by glorifying him and humbling myself before him?

- Ask for grace to live like Daniel separate from the world and in the fear of God. Daniel had a clear understanding of what it meant to live in the world but not be of it. We must pray for the same wisdom to not compromise with worldliness and to live faithfully and beautifully with unbelievers in a world of sin.

- Ask for grace to have a higher regard for what the Lord thinks about you than for what people think of you. Daniel continued to honor those from whom he had separated himself and to honor God's people, but most importantly, he continued to seek the favor of the Lord. For, as Psalm 30:5 says, "in his favour is life."

- Ask for grace to be faithful in big and little things, remembering that the world is checking out your integrity. Alexander Maclaren wrote, "The world takes its notions of God, most of all, from the people who say that they belong to God's family. They read us a great deal more than they read the Bible. They see us; they only hear about Jesus Christ" (*First and Second Peter and First John* [New York: Eaton and Maines, 1910], 105). Remember, too, what Luke 16:10 says, "He that is faithful in that which is least is faithful also in much: and he that is unjust in the least is unjust also in much."

- Ask for grace to be courageous in standing firm for biblical principles. Ask the Lord to give you what you need to dare to stand alone, as Daniel did, against sin. The future of the church depends on more people who will dare to say no to sin and yes to God.

- Ask the Lord to give you friends who say no to sinful ways. Ask for friends like Shadrach, Meshach, and Abednego. Also, when looking for a mate for life, do not look for one who always says yes. Pray that God may guide you to a partner who has deep respect for the truth and yearns to walk in the fear of the Lord.

- Ask the Lord for a life filled with prayer. You cannot come too often or stay too long at the throne of grace. The Lord asks you to acknowledge him in all your ways, for then he will direct your paths (Prov. 3:6). Pray above all for a conversion through which you have a personal, saving acquaintance with Jesus Christ, the only Savior.

- Ask for grace to refrain from sin. Do not think you can stand firm in your own strength. Pray every morning: "Lord, give me what I need today to avoid temptation but also to remain firm when in the midst of it."

- Ask for grace, like Daniel, to avoid those people, places, and customs that place temptation in your path. Instead of asking, "How far can I go and still not sin?" ask, "How can I stay as far away as possible from sin?"

- Ask for grace to realize the benefits of consistent integrity, remembering that the upright cannot live apart from Christ. They generally have more assurance of their faith than the inconsistent believer (Ps. 15:1–2). They pray with greater liberty, confidence, and joy. Being strengthened in the inner man, they can be bold before God and men. Their end will be peace (Ps. 37:37).

Will Your Life Be Wasted?

Daniel worked in Babylon for more than seventy years without ever losing his resolve and becoming a Babylonian. What did he accomplish during that time? He lived for Christ, yes, but what did he really achieve? You might think that he did not change much. Babylon did not become a believing country, and there was no national reformation. This godless empire was eventually replaced by an equally godless one.

So what did Daniel's faithfulness accomplish? Only eternity will reveal the results of Daniel's life and ours. But we must take the long view, realizing that every thought, every word, every action, and every cup of cold water is significant in God's eyes.

Over the centuries young men and women, like Daniel, have lived outstanding lives for Christ. In themselves, they were nothing. They were sinners like you and me. But by the grace of God, they became shining trophies of God's glory by persevering with integrity to the end of their lives. That same grace is available to every single one of you today.

Before you answer life's big questions, such as who you will marry, what career you will pursue, and what occupation you will enter, answer this one: Will you waste your life, or will you follow God with consistent integrity? Any life but a life lived fully and faithfully for Jesus is a wasted life.

> *Only one life, 'twill soon be past,*
> *Only what's done for Christ will last.*

So what is your life like now? If some God-fearing people followed you around for one week, what would they think about your integrity? Would they approve of what you viewed on the Internet and what you watched on TV? What would they think of the books you read, the text messages you sent, the conversations you had, the music you listened to, and the way you dressed? Would they say that you were walking with consistent godliness, like Daniel in Babylon, or would they say you were compromising with the world every day?

Not too long ago, a Christian pastor from the Far East spoke at a large conference. He said, "You Christians in the West feel sorry for us because of the persecution we are called to endure. We appreciate your prayers and concern, but you should know that we feel sorry for you, for you are in greater danger of succumbing to the enemy than we are. To us, the enemy is obvious; to you, it is subtle. The enemy is trying to frighten us, but he is trying to seduce you. We believe that he is being more successful in the West than in the East."

In the coming years, you will be bombarded with messages from almost every angle: live for money, live for your career, live for the weekend, live for sex, live for cars, live for religion, live for rules, live for reputation. All of these messages boil down to one pathetic plea: waste your life. Will you waste your life? Or will you live for Christ and be amazed at what God can do through you, even though the world may seldom acknowledge you?

Take comfort from realizing that when Jesus died, the world paid scant attention. He seemed to have accomplished little at the cross. In the world's eyes, he died an apparent failure. But just before he died, he rejoiced that he had brought his Father glory on earth by completing the work that he had been given to do.

Dear friends, God has given us a life to live and work to do. Our task is simply to do it prayerfully to the best of our ability and to his glory. Whatever we accomplish or do not accomplish due to our efforts is not all-important. The result of our labors is in God's hands. We are simply called to be faithful, like Daniel: to live with consistent integrity and to do our best with the opportunities he provides us.

Resolve that you will not eat the world's food offered to idols. Purpose in your heart to no longer halt between two opinions. By God's grace, throw down the gauntlet, draw a line in the sand, and stand on the Lord's side to serve him all your life. Jephthah's daughter influenced the daughters of Israel with her sacrificial submission. Bartimaeus influenced the crowd to praise God when he centered on Jesus. Jacob influenced all of Israel through his experience of blessing at Peniel. Daniel influenced Babylon from his position of leadership by his consistent integrity. How are you influencing those around you? How will you influence them?

Pray to God, "Great God of heaven, help me not to waste my life. Help me to side not with worldly and selfish pursuits, but let me with consistent integrity resolve to stand firmly on the side of biblical truth every day and in every trial. Let me dare to be a Daniel who follows thee with consistent integrity."

If we, by God's grace, live like Daniel, God may write this epitaph on our gravestone: "You have brought me glory on earth by completing the work I gave you to do." We will have lived contagious Christian lives. And God, for Christ's sake, will say to us on the Great Day: "Well done, thou good and faithful servant. Enter thou into the joy of thy Lord" (Matt. 25:21).

Study Guide

Study #1: ***Sacrificial Submission***

1. Why does the Holy Spirit use believers' lives so extensively to impact people for good?

2. Consider three believing friends who have most influenced your Christian walk with God for good. List three ways in which their Christian witness became contagious for you.

3. Why is it essential to be a true Christian before our godly conversation can win others to Christ?

4. How can we properly unite God's objective truth of salvation in Christ (outside of us) with subjective truth of salvation in Christ (within us)?

5. Which spiritual discipline do you most need to work on? Why? In dependency on the Spirit, what steps could you implement to employ that discipline more effectively?

6. How can you use the following approaches in evangelizing:

The invitation approach (John 4:7–26)

The testimonial approach (John 9:24–34)

The convicting approach (Acts 2:23, 36)

The intellectual approach (Acts 17:22–31)

The service approach (Acts 9:36)

Can you think of other biblical approaches to use?

7. When did you last share the gospel with someone? How did you do it? How did you feel afterward?

8. What is your greatest obstacle in evangelizing?

   The risk of embarrassment
   The fear of rejection
   The fear of failure
   Inability to express the gospel clearly
   Ignorance
   Other _____

9. If you could truly act on your belief that we are to live every minute of every day loving and serving God and our neighbor, how would your life change?

10. The Israelites inherited great trouble because they initially failed to make a full conquest of the Canaanites. What spiritual lesson should this teach us?

11. What encouragements can we glean from the fact that God often uses surprising people, such as Jephthah, to forward his agenda and kingdom?

12. When should we make vows to God? Why should we be careful doing so?

13. A young Christian woman comes to you for advice. She once was in love with a Christian young man. When the relationship started unraveling, she became distraught, and begged God to intervene to resolve the problems. While pleading in prayer, she vowed to God that if it was God's will that this relationship would not last, she would remain single forever. The relationship did not last. She now wonders some years later if there is any way she can be relieved of this vow or is she now bound to a celibate life?

14. How was the submission of Jephthah's daughter superior to the submission of Jephthah himself?

15. How can each of the five steps of submission expounded in this chapter assist you in augmenting the contagiousness of your life?

16. Why do we experience such great peace when we submit unconditionally to God?

17. Why and how is Christ's submission the foundation of our submission?

Study #2: ***Christ-centeredness***

1. Give five reasons why it is essential to be a *Christ-centered* believer.

2. Why does the conversion of a single unconverted person far surpass the external beauty of Jericho and every other city in the world?

3. Spiritually speaking, how is our poverty even worse than Bartimaeus's physical poverty?

4. What evidences did Bartimaeus show that his needs went beyond physical sight? How do these evidences parallel those of sinners who become spiritually concerned?

5. What kinds of obstacles have you experienced in coming to Jesus? How were those obstacles resolved?

6. What should we learn from the crowd first rebuking Bartimaeus and then, only moments later, inviting him to come to Jesus upon Jesus' own command?

7. Explain how Bartimaeus's casting aside of his outer garment is a beautiful picture of how a sinner casts away all his own righteousness and pride in coming to Jesus.

8. What did Bartimaeus mean when he called Jesus "Rabboni," and how did that confession reveal his willingness to surrender his entire life to Jesus? What implications does this have for us today?

9. Why didn't Bartimaeus return home after being healed by Jesus? What spiritual applications can be drawn from his following Jesus "in the way"?

10. Why is following Jesus so challenging for us? Who and what can help us meet the challenges involved?

11. List ten ways in which believers glorify God. How could you better glorify God in your personal life, in your family, at church, at work, and in society?

12. You're sitting on an airplane next to a nominal Christian who has no experiential acquaintance with Christ. You want to glorify God by speaking with him about his spiritual needs. How would you begin such a conversation?

13. Why is it so tragic for sinners to let Jesus pass by without crying out for his mercy? If you are still unconverted, what excuses do you have for remaining in that dreadful state? Why do these excuses hold no weight?

Study #3: *Contagious Blessing*

1. Have you experienced an encounter with God, such that you could say, "God met with me and blessed me there"?

2. Have you ever wrestled with God in the dark night of discouragement, guilt, loss, temptation, pain, and fear? What lessons have you learned from wrestling with God in times of great need?

3. How does the combination of solitude and strife promote wrestling with God and, ultimately, spiritual maturation? How has this taken place in your life?

4. How can we persevere with God in wrestling prayer? Why do we so often fail to do so? How does this lack negatively impact the modern church?

5. Why did the Angel only touch Jacob's thigh and not crush it? Why weren't all of Jacob's bones put out of joint? What lessons does this teach us?

6. Explain how the Angel's crippling touch was really an act of the relentless, crippling grace of God Almighty. If you truly believed this explanation, how would you view your afflictions differently from this day forward?

7. Explain how both God and Jacob won the wrestling match. What implications does this have experientially for your own spiritual walk with God?

8. Have you ever experienced that when you become what you are before God—a lost sinner—God becomes for you what he is: a glorious Savior and Lord? What was the fruit of this experience in your own life?

9. How can Christians exercise contagious power (1) with God and (2) with man? What kind of power is this?

10. What does it really mean to be "blessed by God"?

11. How does a sunrise convey the idea of power? What implications should that have for us as we walk in the strength of the Son of righteousness?

12. How is it possible to embrace pain and to even thank God for it? How can we experience both pain and progress simultaneously in the Christian life?

13. What comfort can you glean from the fact that God repeatedly calls himself "the God of Jacob" in the Scriptures?

Study #4: ***Consistent Integrity***

1.   What is Christian integrity?

2.   What temptations do you confront that attack
     your integrity? Do you resolve in your heart
     to fight against them? What steps could you
     take to help you fulfill your resolution more
     consistently?

3.   Why are we prone to compromise with the
     world and desensitize our own consciences?
     What excuses are we using that tend to desen-
     sitize our consciences and keep us from making
     and keeping Daniel's resolution?

4.   Ralph Erskine said that we should use two tac-
     tics in warding off temptation: fight and flight.
     Where we are strong, we should fight the temp-
     tation head on; where we are weak, we should
     flee it as fast as we can. How could this combi-
     nation of tactics assist you in battling your own
     set of temptations?

5. How can the ten pointers provided to fight against peer pressure be helpful for you in this daily battle? How can you be a force of positive peer pressure on those around you?

6. What does it mean to be jealous for God's reputation and jealous for our own soul? What implications should that have for our daily lives?

7. Why does God try our faith?

8. List five lessons that we learn, by the Spirit's grace, when we are in the midst of trials.

9. What ramifications does this statement have for you: "God does not promise us an easy life, but he does promise us a blessed life"? How can this comfort you?

10. How could Daniel persevere with consistent integrity for more than seventy years in a highly charged, political world without falling or giving up?

11. Are you striving, by grace, to live a life of consistent integrity? If not, what will you do about it? If so, how can you improve in this area?